本书为国家社会科学基金艺术学重大项目"国有表演艺术院团体制改革现状调查与发展路径研究（项目号13ZD05）"研究成果。

This book is the research result of "Research on the Current Situation of System Reform and Development Path of State Performance Art Troupes", Major Project of National Social Science Foundation in Arts.

中国演艺市场
发展报告（汉英对照）

MARKET DEVELOPMENT REPORT
OF CHINESE PERFORMING ARTS
(CHINESE AND ENGLISH VERSION)

李小牧　朱克宁　主　　编
李嘉珊　潘　燕　执行主编

社会科学文献出版社
SOCIAL SCIENCES ACADEMIC PRESS (CHINA)

目　录

第三部分 附录

CONTENTS

Part Ⅲ   Appendix

序　言

古丝绸之路通过贸易连接起亚欧非人类文明。今天，当我们以民心相通为基础推进"一带一路"建设之时，离不开文化的传播与文明的对话，文化贸易成为切实有效联通"一带一路"的人文纽带，"一带一路"沿线国家也必然是中国开展演艺对外贸易的重要区域。伴随中国整体经济实力的增强，2013年中国文化产品出口总值达601亿美元，成为全球最大的文化产品出口国，中国演艺"走出去"也实现了从文化交流向演艺贸易的转变——包括演艺在内的文化产品与服务的对外贸易。中国演艺事业迎来了优化升级和提质增效的新机遇。

以演艺为代表的文化服务贸易的比重将随着文化服务经济的发展不断增大，中国演艺对外贸易结构将进一步优化，演艺服务在商业存在、境外消费、跨境交付以及自然人流动等模式上均会有良性发展；随着中国对"一带一路"沿线国家投资、贸易的增长以及中国取得的巨大成就，这些国家对中国文化的好奇心持续增强、对中国人民的生活方式等方面的兴趣会陡然提升、对中国演艺产品和服务的需求将呈现爆发性增长。中国参与演艺贸易的主体将更加多元，中阿文化部长论坛、中国与东盟10+1文化部长会议等政府层面的机制保障助推了国际文化合作机制的完善，也会吸引越来越多国有和民营院团、社会组织、演艺中介机构以及个人等相关主体加入演艺贸易的行列中。目前中国已经在11个"一带一路"沿线国家设立中国文化中心，中国也将作为连接"一带一路"沿线国家的主体在发展演艺贸易中发挥更好的平台作用。

"一带一路"建设也为中国国内演艺市场的发展升级创造机遇。一方面，中国不断增长的演艺消费需求将逐步外溢到"一带一路"沿线国家；另一方面，更为重要的是中国演艺产品与服务必将更多地参与国际竞争，通过"需求－供给传导机制"倒逼国内演艺产业供给侧深化改革，演艺市场同步完善，从而催生出高品质的演艺产品与服务。国内演艺市场的日臻完善将通过可交易的演艺产品与服务自信表达中华文化，引导更多国民增强对中国文化的高度认同和深刻理解，有效实现中华文化的跨时代沟通。

与此同时，文化投资将为中国演艺贸易注入持久动力。中国对外文化投资的步伐不断加快，对外文化投资方式将日益多元，设立海外分公司、跨国并购和签署合作协议等都成为企业对外文化投资的重要方式。对外文化投资主体也将更加多样，不仅局限于文化企业本身，更多实行多角化经营的公司也将文化产业视为其重要的进军领域，制造业、地产、金融等领域的规模企业将凭借其雄厚的经济实力和资金储备更多地参与到对外文化投资当中。目前中国对"一带一路"沿线国家非金融类直接投资超过 500 亿美元，并在 20 个沿线国家建设的56 个境外经贸合作区累计投资超过 185 亿美元；"一带一路"沿线已有的投资流量将推动已经与"一带一路"沿线国家发生贸易往来或产业投资的中国跨国企业更加迅速地实现资金的跨产业迁移，融入当地演艺市场，为中国演艺产业走入世界演艺市场搭建桥梁。

值得注意的是，"一带一路"沿线国家文化产业的发展大多起步较晚，发展速度缓慢，挑战与机遇并存，中国与"一带一路"沿线国家的演艺产业合作需要建立各方共同建设、共担风险、共享收益的利益共同体，需要借助市场力量，最大限度地促进生产要素有序流动、资源高效配置，文化市场才能深度融合。"一带一路"建设注定是一场全球性、高水平、深层次的伟业，在这条和平之路、繁荣之路、开放之路、创新之路、文明之路上，包括演艺在内的文化贸易必将发挥其独特优势，切实联通"一带一路"人文纽带，"无论相隔多远，坚持相向而行，就能走出一条相遇相知、共同发展之路，走向幸福安宁和谐美好的远方"。

与其他文化产品和服务相比，演艺产品和服务具有受科技现代化的冲击最小、资本现代化程度较低、产业规模空间狭窄等突出的经济特征。同时，它艺术地承载着特定国家和地区的核心文化价值，在愉悦的欣赏与体验中，使人们潜移默化地感知与认同，并接受情感教育、舒缓压力，因此演艺文化贸易是实现文化对外传播的智慧路径。《中国演艺市场发展报告》正是在"一带一路"倡议为中国演艺对外贸易带来了新机遇之际，由国家文化发展国际战略研究院专门组织团队编写而成，以中英双语向海内外呈现"十二五"这一中国文化产业发展的重要时期内中国演艺市场的发展变迁，并对 2016 年中国演艺产业和演艺对外贸易的发展情况进行梳理和深入剖析。希望此书能够成为了解中国演艺产业及其对外贸易的一扇窗口，在继续服务中国演艺对外贸易发展的同时，让全球更多国家和地区的政府、企业、学术机构和人民发现中国演艺市场的巨大消费潜力，发掘演艺产业的国际合作空间，推动中国与"一带一路"沿线国家共绘演艺贸易蓝图。

编者

2018 年春

第一部分

"十二五"期间演艺产业发展概况

　　"十二五"期间（2011~2015 年）"节俭令"影响下的中国演艺市场悄然发生变化，曾经看似繁荣的演艺市场正在挤掉泡沫，向着更加健全和完善方向发展。在演出市场形势变化、竞争日趋激烈的新形势下，部分演艺院团积极抓住机遇，扩大消费人群，收到了较好的社会效益和经济效益。"十二五"期间，为推动文化发展繁荣，国家出台了一系列优化文化发展环境的利好政策，如国务院《关于加快发展对外文化贸易的意见》，文化部、中国人民银行、财政部《关于深入推进文化金融合作的意见》，财政部、国家税务总局《关于小型微利企业所得税优惠政策有关问题的通知》，文化部、工业和信息化部、财政部《关于大力支持小微文化企业发展的实施意见》等。这些政策解决了文化企业在生存和发展中存在的实际问题，也为文化企业带来了新的发展机遇。

　　文化体制改革持续稳步推进，国有文艺院团体制改革仍是文化工作重点。扶持文化艺术发展的投入方式大有转变，由原来的直接拨款，转变为通过政府购买服务、原创剧目补贴、以奖代补等方式，扶持演艺企业创作生产，增强其面向市场服务群众的能力。在文艺创作导向方面，习近平总书记在文艺工作座谈会上的重要讲话为今后文艺创作指明了方向，引导文艺工作者认识所担负的历史使命和责任，坚持以人民为中心的创作导向，努力创作更多无愧于时代的优秀作品。政府在行政管理上将进一步简政放权和加强审批规范相结合，在激发市场活力的同时，使得行政管理更加规范、透明、公正。

从国际看，世界多极化、经济全球化、文化多样化、社会信息化深入发展，文化在国际交往中的地位和作用更加凸显，"一带一路"倡议带来了诸多文化合作机制和保障，为包括演艺在内的中国文化产业及其对外贸易创造了无限可能。同时，世界范围内各种思想文化交流交融交锋更加频繁，综合国力竞争更加激烈，文化安全形势更加复杂，提高国家文化软实力、增强国际话语权的任务日趋紧迫。作为文化重要组成的演艺产业迎来了重大发展机遇，也面临诸多挑战。

"十二五"时期的中国演艺业，处于不断发展繁荣又逐步升级的状态，整体不断向着更加优化、更加稳定的市场结构方向发展。

一 营业规模不断增长

（一）演艺机构数量显著上升

"十二五"期间演艺业机构数量有了明显增长。2011年共有7055个艺术表演团体机构、1429个艺术表演场馆机构；2012年共有7321个艺术表演团体机构、1279个艺术表演场馆机构，2012年艺术表演团体机构数比2011年增长了3.77%、2012年艺术表演场馆机构数比2011年下降了10.50%；2013年共有8180个艺术表演团体机构、1344

个艺术表演场馆机构，比2012年分别增长了11.73%、5.08%；2014年共有8769个艺术表演团体机构、1338个艺术表演场馆机构，2014年艺术表演团体机构数比2013年增长了7.20%、2014年艺术表演场馆机构数比2013年下降了0.45%；2015年共有10787个艺术表演团体机构、2143个艺术表演场馆机构，比2014年分别增长了23.01%、60.16%（见图1-1、图1-2）。

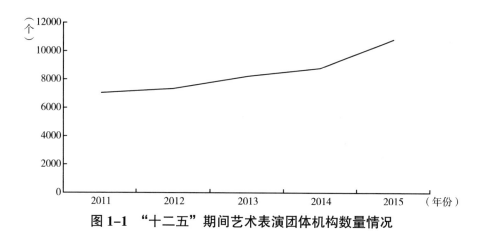

图1-1 "十二五"期间艺术表演团体机构数量情况

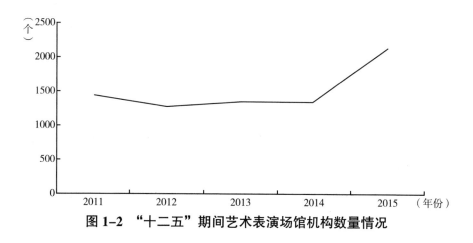

图1-2 "十二五"期间艺术表演场馆机构数量情况

　　总体而言，无论艺术表演团体机构还是艺术表演场馆机构数量都保持了较为稳定的增长趋势，"十二五"期间演艺机构数量整体从 2011 年的 8484 个增加到 2015 年的 12930，年平均增长率达到11.54%，增长速度最快的 2015 年达到了 27.93%（见图 1-3）。①

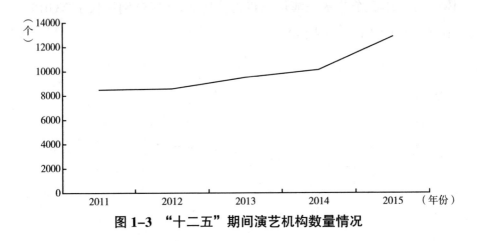

图 1-3　"十二五"期间演艺机构数量情况

（二）演出场次波动中攀升

　　"十二五"期间演出场次在波动中增长。2011 年全国艺术表演团体共演出 155 万场次，艺术表演场馆共演出 56.2 万场次；2012 年全国艺术表演团体共演出 135 万场次，艺术表演场馆共演出 57.5 万场次，2012 年全国艺术表演团体演出的场次比 2011 年下降了 12.90%、2012年全国艺术表演场馆演出场次比 2011 年增加了 2.31%；2013 年全国艺术表演团体共演出 165 万场次，艺术表演场馆共演出 82.9 万场次，

---

① 数据来源：国家统计局社会科技和文化产业统计司、中宣部文化体制改革和发展办公室《中国文化及相关产业统计年鉴 2015》，中国统计出版社。

分别比 2012 年增加了 22.22%、44.17%；2014 年全国艺术表演团体共演出 174 万场次，艺术表演场馆共演出 78.1 万场次，2014 年全国艺术表演团体演出的场次比 2013 年增加了 5.45%、2014 年全国艺术表演场馆演出场次比 2013 年下降了 5.79%；2015 年全国艺术表演团体共演出 211 万场次，艺术表演场馆共演出 106.5 万场次，分别比 2014 年增加了 21.26%、36.36%（见图 1-4、图 1-5）。

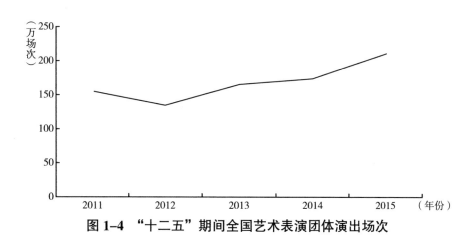

图 1-4 "十二五"期间全国艺术表演团体演出场次

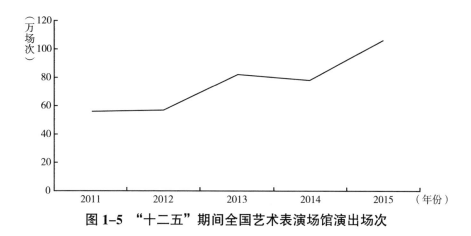

图 1-5 "十二五"期间全国艺术表演场馆演出场次

艺术表演团体和艺术表演场馆演出场次都存在不同程度的波动，因而也导致了"十二五"期间演出总场次在2012年的小幅下降，但总体仍保持了平稳增长。"十二五"期间演出总场次从2012年的192.5万场次到2015年的317.5万场次，年平均增长率达到11.89%，增速最高的2013年达到了28.78%（见图1-6）。[①]

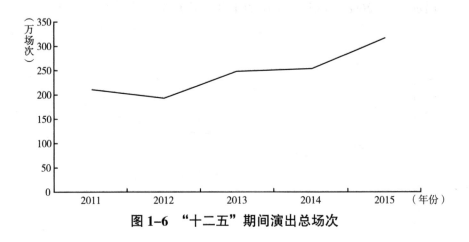

图1-6 "十二五"期间演出总场次

（三）观众人次持续增加

"十二五"期间演艺观众人次同样逐步攀升，2011年观众总人次为81512万人（其中艺术表演团体74585万人、艺术表演场馆6927万人）；2012年观众总人次为88904.7万人（其中艺术表演团体82805万人，艺术表演场馆6099.7万人），比2011年增加9.07%；2013年观众总人次为97840.3万人（其中艺术表演团体90064万人，艺术表演场馆7776.3万人），比2012年增加10.05%；2014年观众总人次为97864.4万人（其中艺术表演团体91020万人，艺术表演场馆6844.4万人），

---

① 数据来源：国家统计局社会科技和文化产业统计司、中宣部文化体制改革和发展办公室《中国文化及相关产业统计年鉴》，中国统计出版社。

比 2013 年增加 0.02%；2015 年观众总人次为 106574.4 万人（其中艺术表演团体 95799 万人，艺术表演场馆 10775.4 万人），比 2014 年增加 8.90%。从观众人次的持续增加可以看出，国内越来越多的消费者开始关注、观看演出，市场受众得到不断培育（见图 1-7）。①

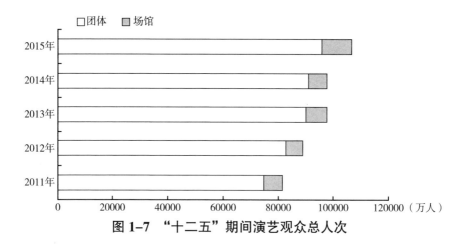

图 1-7 "十二五"期间演艺观众总人次

二 从业人员规模扩大

"十二五"期间演艺从业人员规模增长明显，从 2011 年的 253079 人（其中艺术表演团体从业人员 226599 人，艺术表演剧场从业人员 26480 人）到 2015 年的 348612 人（其中艺术表演团体从业人员 301878 人，艺术表演剧场从业人员 46734 人），五年间演艺从业人员数量增加了近 37.75%，随着国内演艺市场需求的不断增长，从业人员数量的增加有利于演艺生产能力的提升（见图 1-8）。②

① 数据来源：国家统计局社会科技和文化产业统计司、中宣部文化体制改革和发展办公室《中国文化及相关产业统计年鉴》，中国统计出版社。
② 数据来源：国家统计局社会科技和文化产业统计司、中宣部文化体制改革和发展办公室《中国文化及相关产业统计年鉴》，中国统计出版社。

　　"十二五"期间艺术表演团体及场馆就业人数增速明显高于全国就业人数和第三产业就业人数增长速度，基本每年均大幅超过全国就业人数和第三产业就业人数（除 2014 年外），艺术表演团体及场馆就业人数年平均增长 8.58%，而全国就业人数和第三产业就业人数年平均增长幅度仅为 0.34%、4.76%（见图 1-9）。

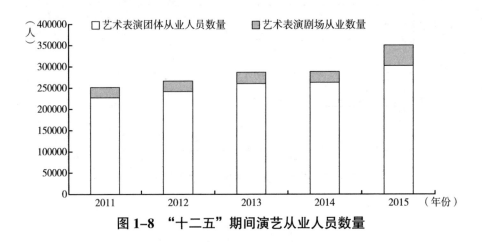

图 1-8 "十二五"期间演艺从业人员数量

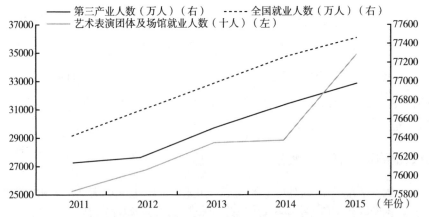

图 1-9 "十二五"期间全国、第三产业、艺术表演团体及场馆就业人数比较
数据来源：人力资源和社会保障部。

三 固定资产投资明显增长

"十二五"期间艺术表演团体实际使用房屋建筑面积快速增长。2011 年实际使用房屋建筑面积为 526 万平方米，2012 年实际使用房屋建筑面积增加到 617 万平方米，比 2011 年增加了 17.30%；2013 年实际使用房屋建筑面积增加到 638 万平方米，比 2012 年增加了 3.40%；2014 年实际使用房屋建筑面积增加到 716 万平方米，比 2013 年增加了 12.23%；2015 年实际使用房屋建筑面积增加到 800 万平方米，比 2014 年增加了 11.73%。艺术表演团体实际使用房屋建筑面积的快速增长也间接反映了"十二五"期间演艺业固定资产投入的增加（见图 1-10）。①

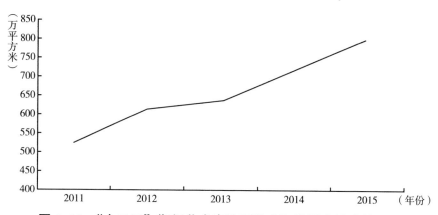

图 1-10 "十二五"期间艺术表演团体实际使用房屋建筑面积

---

① 数据来源：国家统计局社会科技和文化产业统计司、中宣部文化体制改革和发展办公室《中国文化及相关产业统计年鉴》，中国统计出版社。

四 演艺企业利润波动中增长

（一）演出市场总体经济规模略有起伏

"十二五"期间全国演出市场经济规模年平均增长率达 19.82%，增速显著。2011 年全国演出市场经济规模为 233.30 亿元，2012 年增加至 355.90 亿元；2013 年全国演出市场经济规模进一步增长至 463.00 亿元，2014 年全国演出市场经济规模略有下降，为 434.32 亿元，2015 年回升至 446.59 亿元（见图 1–11）。[①]

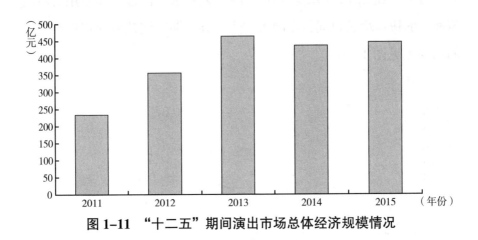

图 1–11 "十二五"期间演出市场总体经济规模情况

（二）演出票房收入结构性波动

"十二五"期间全国演出票房收入（含专业剧场[②]演出，大型

---

① 数据来源：中国演出行业协会《中国演出市场年度报告》；2013 年起剧场全年补贴收入和娱乐演出收入纳入演出市场总体经济规模统计范畴。

② 专业剧场指为演出活动提供专业演出场地及服务的演出场所。

演唱会、音乐节演出,旅游演出,演艺场馆娱乐演出)总体呈增长趋势。2011 年全国演出票房收入达 105.30 亿元,2012 年比上一年增长 28.2%,达到 135.00 亿元;2013 年比 2012 年增长了 25.0%,达到 168.79 亿元;经过两年快速增长后全国演出票房收入于 2013 年出现 12.1% 的小幅下跌,减少至 148.32 亿元;2015 年演全国演出票房收入又上涨了 9.0%,回升至 161.72 亿元(见图 1-12 和表 1-1)。

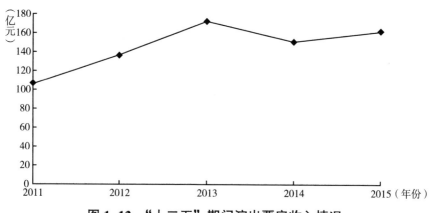

图 1-12 "十二五"期间演出票房收入情况

表 1-1 "十二五"期间各类演出票房收入分布

单位:亿元

年份	总收入	专业剧场演出	大型演唱会、音乐节演出	旅游演出	演艺场馆娱乐演出
2011	105.30	36.70	25.50	27.80	15.30
2012	135.00	61.20	13.30	32.70	27.80
2013	168.79	65.37	21.36	61.20	20.86
2014	148.32	66.09	25.69	38.37	18.17
2015	161.72	70.68	31.80	35.17	24.07

数据来源:中国演出行业协会《中国演出市场年度报告》。

"十二五"期间在演出票房总收入较平稳增长的同时，各类别演出票房收入呈现明显波动。其中增长最平稳同时也是票房收入最高的是专业剧场演出，波动最大的是旅游演出票房收入，分别在 2013 和 2014 年出现较大幅度的增长和下跌。大型演唱会、音乐节演出票房收入和演艺场馆娱乐演出票房收入此消彼长、规模相当（见图 1-13）。"十二五"期间演出票房收入结构变化见图 1-14。

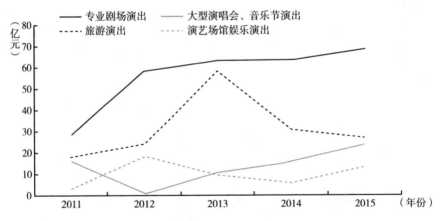

图 1-13 "十二五"期间各类演出票房收入情况

数据来源：中国演出行业协会《中国演出市场年度报告》。

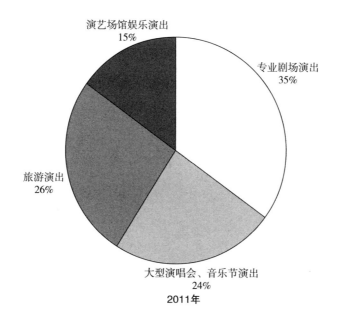

2011年

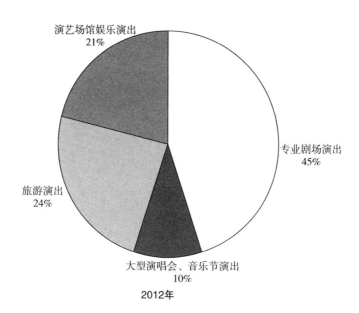

2012年

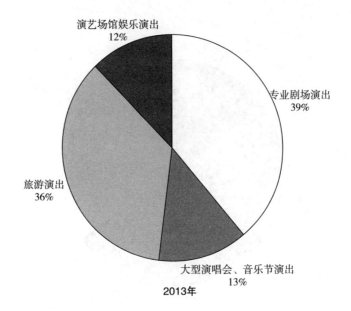

2013年

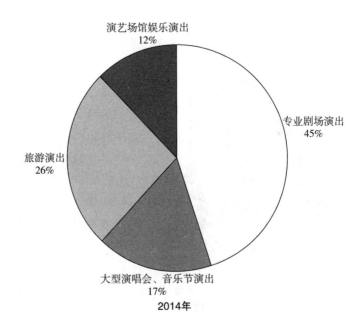

2014年

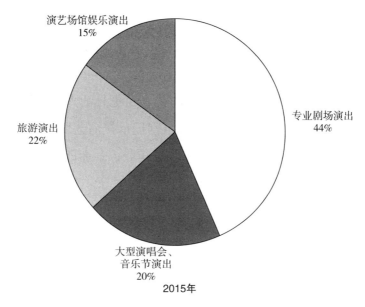

演艺场馆娱乐演出
15%

旅游演出
22%

专业剧场演出
44%

大型演唱会、
音乐节演出
20%

2015年

图1-14 "十二五"期间演出票房收入结构变化

数据来源：中国演出行业协会《中国演出市场年度报告》。

（三）艺术表演团体与剧场收入占比不均

"十二五"期间国内演艺收入大幅增长，年增长率达19.84%，艺术表演团体始终是演艺业创收主体，艺术表演团体收入占比均在75%以上。2011年演艺总收入达到1806362万元（其中艺术表演团体收入1540263万元，艺术表演剧场收入266099万元），2012年演艺总收入达2528683万元（其中艺术表演团体收入2310460万元，艺术表演剧场收入218223万元），比2011年增加39.99%；2013年演艺总收入达3226627万元（其中艺术表演团体收入2800266万元，艺术表演剧场收入426361万元），比2012年增加27.60%；2014年演艺总收入达2667745万元（其中艺术表演团体收入2264046万元，艺术表演剧场收入403699万元），比2013年下降17.32%；2015年演艺总收入达 3444129 万元（其中艺术表演团体收入 2576499 万元，艺术表演剧场收入 867630 万元），比 2014 年增加 29.10%。"十二五"期间演艺收入变化与观众人次的变化基本一致（见图 1–15）。

"十二五"期间演艺团体相比演艺场馆更具活力，剧目的创作生产动力更强，而演艺场馆主要靠出租剧场承接演艺团体的演出创收，造成了演艺团体收入始终远高于演艺场馆收入；而即使是在演艺收入中占比较大的演艺团体，其利润率并不高，"十二五"期间演艺团体收入的利润率平均仅为 9%（见图 1–16）。

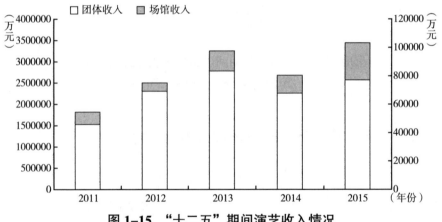

图 1–15 "十二五"期间演艺收入情况

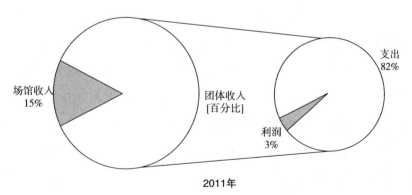

2011年

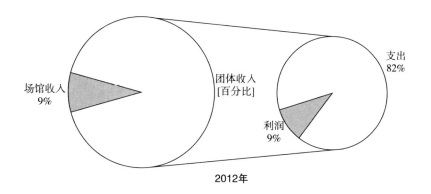

2012年

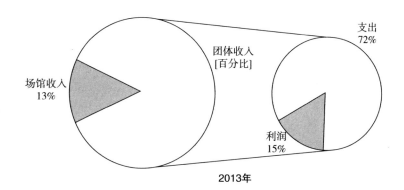

2013年

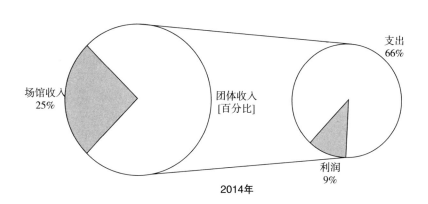

2014年

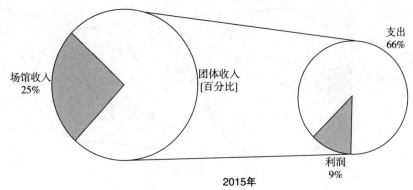

场馆收入
25%

团体收入
[百分比]

支出
66%

利润
9%

2015年

图1-16　十二五期间演艺收入占比

数据来源：国家统计局社会科技和文化产业统计司、中宣部文化体制改革和发展办公室：《中国文化及相关产业统计年鉴》，中国统计出版社。

第二部分

2016 年中国演艺市场发展报告

随着中国进入"十三五"新时期，文化体制改革进入深化发展阶段，文化产业对国民经济的贡献越发凸显，"十三五"时期文化发展改革规划等一系列提高文化发展的质量和效益、推动社会主义文化大发展大繁荣的政策法规陆续出台，也使得大力发展对外文化贸易成为中国提高文化开放水平的重要内容。国家发展的国际战略所带来的重大发展机遇使得中国演艺对外贸易迎来了优化升级和快速增长的新机遇。

作为"十三五"开局之年的 2016 年，中国演艺市场整体继续保持着稳健的增长，演艺市场结构仍不稳定，与相关产业融合发展程度加深。一线城市演艺市场辐射全国，带动各地区演艺市场发展的地位和作用已经慢慢凸显，资金也不断涌入演艺市场。在演艺对外贸易方面，国外引进剧目依然是推动中国演艺院团不断学习和提高院团自身建设的助力，演艺市场化运作愈发受到重视，大型文化交流项目逐渐寻求转型。与此同时中国国内开始建立系统的演艺服务平台和基金制度，为演艺院团"走出去"提供保障。

一 2016 年中国演艺市场发展特点

2016 年，全国演出场次共计 183.1 万场，市场经济规模达 469.22 亿元，近六年来虽然演出场次存在一定波动，但演出市场规模整体呈稳定增长态势（见图 2-1）。^① 在稳定的市场环境中，中国演艺业呈现出跨界融合，由一线城市辐射全国等特点，各地演艺市场联系越发紧密。

图 2-1　2011~2016 年全国演出场次及演出市场经济规模

（一）演艺市场效益连续增长

2016 年演出市场总体经济规模 469.22 亿元，相较于 2015 年的经济规模 446.59 亿元，同比增长 5.07%，经济规模自 2014 年以来已经连续三年增长。其中演艺票房收入（含旅游被分账收入，见图 2-2）

---

① 数据来源：中国演出行业协会《2016 年中国演出市场年度报告》。

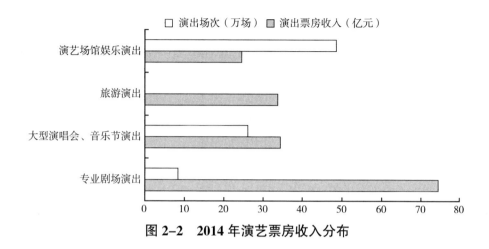

图 2-2　2014 年演艺票房收入分布

168.09 亿元，比 2015 年上升 3.93%；农村演出收入 24.24 亿元，比 2015 年上升 8.60%；娱乐演出收入 71.03 亿元，比 2015 年上升 2.00%；演出衍生产品及赞助收入 31.57 亿元，比 2015 年上升 7.97%；经营主体配套设施及其他服务收入 54.54 亿元，比 2015 年降低 1.25%；政府补贴收入（不含农村惠民补贴收入）119.74 亿元，比 2015 年上升 10.42%。

2016 年全国演艺市场总体收入已经超过 2013 年 463 亿元的峰值，创造了 6 年来演艺市场经济规模新高，演出场地也少见的连续三年呈现增长趋势，这对于经常出现波动的中国演艺市场实属难得，足以体现近年来中国演艺市场整体保持住了稳增长的态势。平稳的经济环境为全国演艺院团尝试更多的创新与探索提供了保障，也使全国演艺市场抵御风险的能力增强。

（二）各类演出发展独具特色

2016 年全国演出场所共演出 183.1 万场次，比 2015 年的 172.32

万场次增长了 6.26%，2011 年至今全国演艺市场演出总场次数量波动幅度很小，但具体到某一门类的演出场次波动频繁，演出收入 2014年以前升降频繁，2014 年之后方才稳定下来，演出场次和演出收入都保持小幅波动或正向增长（见图 2-3、图 2-4）。[①]

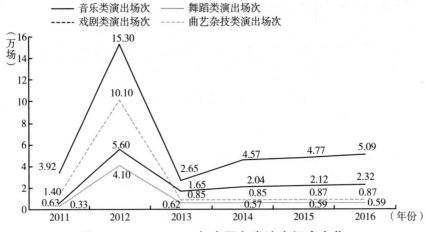

图 2-3　2011~2016 年全国各类演出场次变化

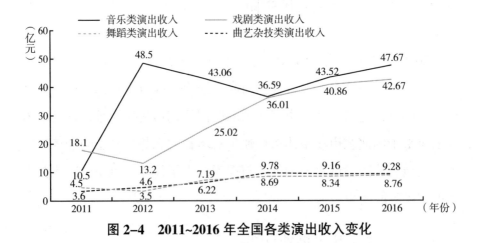

图 2-4　2011~2016 年全国各类演出收入变化

---

① 数据来源：中国演出行业协会《2016 年中国演出市场年度报告》。

1. 音乐类演出

（1）音乐会

2016年音乐会的市场表现十分突出，专业剧场演出场次和票房收入均有较大幅度的提升，艺术普及和市场培育效果显现（见表2-1）。

表2-1　2015~2016年音乐会演出市场对比情况

类别	2015年	2016年	增长率（%）
场次（万场）	1.93	2.11	9.33
平均票价（元）	143	150	↑
上座率（%）	71	85	↑
观众人数（万人）	547.51	627.73	14.65
票房收入（亿元）	11.72	12.79	9.13

国际交响乐团来华演出高水平、高密度。2016年，诸多国际高水平交响乐团纷纷来华演出，几乎每个月都有具有世界影响力的乐团造访，其中包括维也纳爱乐乐团、费城交响乐团、圣彼得堡爱乐乐团、德国德累斯顿爱乐乐团、波兰华沙交响乐团、旧金山交响乐团等。仅2016年1月国家大剧院就有祖宾·梅塔、里卡尔多·穆蒂、克利斯朵夫·艾森巴赫和帕特里克·朗格分别率领以色列爱乐乐团、芝加哥交响乐团、德国石荷州音乐节乐团和维也纳广播交响乐团演出。

世界名团频频造访，一方面得益于中国日渐成熟和不断完善的演出场所，拥有了邀请名团来华演出的经济实力和设施条件；另一方面得益于观众规模扩大以及观众音乐素养和欣赏水平的提升，2016年音乐会观众人数较2015年增长了14.65%，上座率达到了85%。

二三线城市音乐会市场兴起。伴随各地剧院完成建设及"北上广"一线城市音乐会市场的饱和与竞争，许多音乐会项目资源向二三线城市转移。例如，北京交响乐团在2016年下半年与保利院线合作，在常熟、宜兴、昆山、武汉、长沙等14个城市巡演；钢琴家李云迪也选择了惠州、威海、潍坊、舟山、昆山等城市作为音乐会的巡演地；指挥家余隆和音乐家马友友、吴彤则与西安、兰州、乌鲁木齐等城市的乐团合作进行演出。名家名团在二三线城市的演出进一步拓展了音乐会市场，培育更多观众。

古典与现代融合，传统与时尚碰撞，音乐会内容不断创新。音乐会在演出内容上不局限于传统经典曲目，变得更加多元，以电影音乐、动漫音乐、游戏音乐为主题的音乐会吸引了新的观众群体。跨界混搭也成为音乐会演出创新的一种方式，例如，北京民族乐团推出的多媒体情景音乐会《五行》用笛、箫、埙等民族乐器配合人声、打击乐、电子乐等营造视听效果；上海音乐厅推出的"乐无穷"音乐季中将古典音乐与电子乐混搭，将音乐与舞蹈组合，对戏曲音乐进行全新演绎。

创新为音乐会演出在信息时代生发了新的关注点，如上海馨忆民族室内乐团演出的"玲珑国乐"民乐音乐会允许观众现场拍照，民乐演奏的《机器猫》和迈克尔·杰克逊代表作 *Smooth Criminal* 被传到网上后引发网友关注；彩虹室内合唱团音乐会上的返场曲目《张士超你到底把我家钥匙放在哪里了》《感觉身体被掏空》以诙谐幽默写实成为网络爆款，引发热议。这样契合年轻观众口味的创新，发掘、培育了更多观众。

（2）演唱会

2016年演唱会、音乐节演出场次0.21万场，较2015年上升10.53%，票房收入34.88亿元，较2015年上升9.69%。

明星演唱会成本高，推高演唱会票价。据统计，2016 年明星在大型体育场馆举办演唱会的最低平均票价约为 300 元，最高平均票价约为 1300 元，一线具有票房号召力的明星演唱会票价更为突出，例如，周杰伦巡演北京站票价为 580~2280 元、张学友巡演北京站票价为 580~1880 元、陈奕迅巡演北京站票价为 380~1980 元，备受关注的王菲 2016 年上海演唱会票价定为 1800~7800 元。

造成演唱会高票价的直接原因是投入成本高，除了高昂的明星及其团队出场费外，场地租金、舞台搭建、灯光音响、安保费用等都是大型演唱会的必须支出，一场演唱会投入成本需要几百万至千万不等，高成本最终要通过高票价转嫁给消费者，此外工作票、赠票等带来的隐形成本也间接推高票价。

低投入低风险剧场演唱会兴起。近两年。相对小众的歌手在剧场举办演唱会成为趋势，例如，陈绮贞、陈粒、逃跑计划、杭盖乐队等歌手与乐队的 2016 年巡演均选择在专业剧场中举办。相对于大型体育场馆，在剧场举办演唱会的优势在于投入较低、成本可控、风险较小，一场演唱会投入在几十万至一百万。据统计，2016 年剧场内演唱会最低平均票价约为 180 元，最高平均票价约为 800 元。

对于大多数歌手，在市场号召力不足以支撑大型场馆演出的情况下，举办剧场演唱会是一条传播音乐、培育受众的新途径。这就需要歌手放下"非大型演唱会不可"的观念，需要运营机构放下"三年不开张，开张吃三年"的谋利心态，合理规划，薄利多销，丰富文化产品供给类型。

互联网深度介入演唱会运营。互联网深入演唱会运营，在线直播成为演唱会的必选项，对应这一部分的版权收入也成为演唱会重要的盈利渠道。选择在线观看演唱会直播的观众人数大幅增长，腾讯视频

LiveMusic 2016 年直播演唱会 400 场，累计播放量达到 20 亿次，覆盖受众超过 6 亿；在其平台直播的王菲"幻乐一场"演唱会实现了在全球 166 个国家同步直播，当晚的直播总观看人数超过 2000 万，累计总播放量达 3.4 亿。

由新媒体"新音乐产业观察"发布的《2016 年中国音乐市场消费报告》显示，32% 的受访者会选择观看付费演唱会在线直播，2016 年乐视音乐直播的华晨宇火星演唱会单场付费 50 元，上海和深圳两场演唱会直播付费观看人数超过 13 万次。

据中国互联网络信息中心发布的《第 39 次中国互联网络发展状况统计报告》显示，在视频直播领域，2016 年演唱会直播市场规模的发展速度仅次于游戏直播。面对优质内容资源有限、版权竞争激烈的状况，各直播平台在提升用户体验、完善付费业务、进行线下布局、加强商业化运作等方面发挥各自优势，通过内容导入用户，多样运作实现流量变现。例如，乐视音乐参与主办李宇春 2016 "野蛮生长"演唱会，随门票配套赠送易到用车代金券和乐视超级体育会员卡，实现线下门票的线上增值服务；周笔畅 Boom!+ 北京演唱会则推出了定制手机，随手机赠送门票，定制手机中包含其无损音乐、专属信息推送、新闻日历、独家定制闹钟铃声等。

（3）音乐节

2016 年演唱会、音乐节演出场次 0.21 万场，较 2015 年上升 10.53%，票房收入 34.88 亿元，较 2015 年上升 9.69%。

场次增长，新晋音乐节数量增多。经过 2015 年的调整期，2016 年音乐节场次超过 500 场，增长显著。仅草莓音乐节就在全国 22 个城市举办。除整体场次增长外，2016 年出现了多个首次举办的音乐节，包括 echo 回声音乐节、山谷民谣音乐节等在内的 20 余个新晋音乐节。音乐节市场显著增长的原因，一是音乐行业整体的发展与提升，特别是受益于数字版权管理规范带来的原创提升和产业重构，现场演出成为音乐变现的重要方式；二是音乐节商业模式的完善让资本看好音乐节的发展前景，例如，echo 回声获光线传媒 3000 万美元 C 轮融资，《野马现场》获明嘉资本 A 轮千万级融资，丛林文化获青松基金、联想之星千万级天使轮融资，资本的投入驱动音乐节扩张升级；三是音乐节成为举办地文化名片和文化竞争力的一个标志，得到了地方政府的支持。

音乐节市场进入垂直细分阶段。垂直类别音乐节的增长是 2016 年音乐节市场的突出特点，包括以 INTRO 电子音乐节、MTA 天漠音乐节等为代表的电子音乐节，以山谷民谣音乐节、新青年民谣音乐节等为代表的民谣音乐节，以 JZ 爵士音乐节、北山爵士音乐节等为代表的爵士音乐节。音乐节市场的垂直细分突破了音乐节同质化的困局，是音乐节内容从"大而全"向"小而精"升级发展的新阶段。

2. 舞蹈类演出

2016 年专业剧场舞蹈演出场次 0.5941 万场，较 2015 年略有增长，票房收入 8.76 亿元，较 2015 年上升 5.04%（见表 2-2）。对比近年音乐会演出和话剧演出的快速增长，舞蹈演出市场发展持续滞缓。

表 2-2　2015~2016 年舞蹈演出市场对比情况

类别	2015 年	2016 年	增长率（%）
场次（万场）	0.59	0.5941	0.24
平均票价（元）	125	140	↑
上座率（%）	44	41	↓
观众人数（万人）	235.14	231.36	-1.61
票房收入（亿元）	8.34	8.76	5.04

（1）中国舞蹈海外市场开拓良好，国际合作紧密

中国舞蹈是除杂技、武术外在国际演出市场上最具商业价值的艺术类型，以中央芭蕾舞团和上海芭蕾舞团为代表的芭蕾舞团，以陶身体剧场、北京现代舞团为代表的现代舞团海外商业演出市场表现良好，逐渐形成了舞团的知名度和中国舞蹈的国际影响力。例如，中央芭蕾舞团舞剧《牡丹亭》2016年在英国巡演13场，票房上佳，赞誉不断；陶身体剧场一年一半以上的时间在海外巡演，平均每年参加19个海外艺术节。

中国舞蹈在国际市场的良好表现，客观上是舞蹈艺术不存在语言障碍，表达方式上受文化差异影响较小；主观上是中国一流的舞蹈团体的编导创作水平和舞台表现能力已经与世界水平看齐，紧密的国际合作创作也为中国舞团开阔国际视野，为打开国际渠道带来了机遇。例如，辽宁芭蕾舞团近三年来先后与南非约翰内斯堡芭蕾舞团合作排演舞剧《天鹅湖》、与法国莱茵芭蕾舞团艺术总监伊万合作现代芭蕾《足迹》、与瑞典艺术家马克合作现代芭蕾《悬崖边缘》、与俄罗斯芭蕾名家格里格洛维奇合作排演《斯巴达克》《罗密欧与朱丽叶》等。

（2）国内观众接受度低制约舞蹈市场发展，观众培养需渗透渐进

从数据上可以看出，舞蹈演出的观众人数呈下降趋势。舞蹈艺术需要观众具备较高的艺术素养才能欣赏理解，"看不懂"使中国观众和舞蹈艺术之间产生隔阂。舞蹈艺术普及教育的欠缺，造成舞蹈市场观众的缺失。舞蹈演出观众的培养需逐步渗透，一方面可加强面向青少年儿童的普及培训，为市场培养未来的观众；另一方面舞团、剧场等机构的舞蹈普及推广工作应从当前观众欣赏水平出发，由浅入深进行解析引导。

舞蹈市场发展缓慢的另一原因出现在艺术创作端，中国舞蹈创作

存在重技术、轻内涵、同质化的问题。舞蹈缺少内涵思想，舞剧拙于叙事表达，演员表现流于程式缺乏个性表现，这些都造成了舞蹈演出不好看、难以形成吸引力、难以培养稳定的受众群等问题。

3. 戏剧类演出

（1）话剧

2016 年专业剧场话剧演出场次 1.51 万场，较 2015 年上升 9.42%，票房收入 24.37 亿元，较 2015 年上升 6.14%（见表 2-3）。话剧有着广泛的观众基础，近年来话剧市场稳步发展，但创作端的薄弱成为制约中国话剧发展的重要因素，弥补原创短板需重视戏剧原创文本的创作和人才队伍的培养。

表 2-3　2015~2016 年话剧演出市场对比情况

类别	2015 年	2016 年	增长率（%）
场次（万场）	1.38	1.51	9.42
平均票价（元）	400	300	↓
上座率（%）	70	85	↑
观众人数（万人）	284.03	320.88	12.97
票房收入（亿元）	22.96	24.37	6.14

场次收入双升，票价降低推高上座率。近年，话剧市场呈现良好的发展态势，话剧市场规模持续增长。2016 年，话剧演出场次和票房收入维持较高的增长率。值得关注的是，2016 年话剧观众人数涨幅显著，较 2015 年增长近 13%，平均票价下降明显，进一步推高了上座率。话剧演出票价下降，一方面得益于政府对文化消费的鼓励和票价补贴；另一方面调低票价也是话剧演出团体自主的一个选择，让利

于观众，以低票价进一步培育市场，以增加演出场次，而不是提高票价，来保证演出收入。

改编剧目不乏精品力作。原创匮乏的短板，让话剧向经典作品寻求创作资源。2016年莎士比亚、汤显祖、老舍、易卜生、契诃夫、迪伦马、丁西林等国内外名家的改编剧目纷纷亮相话剧市场，例如，导演林兆华2016年执导的三部作品，分别是易卜生的《人民公敌》、迪特里希·施万尼茨的《戈多医生或者六个人寻找第十八只骆驼》和莎士比亚的《仲夏夜之梦》；国家话剧院的《比萨斜塔》、北京人艺的《丁西林民国喜剧三则》、陕西人艺的《白鹿原》等。将国内外经典小说、影视、诗歌改编话剧成为院团、编导保证剧目质量和票房号召力的稳妥选择。

引进剧目类型多样、层次丰富。从2014年开始，国外引进剧目数量逐年增加，国家大剧院国际戏剧季、首都剧场精品剧目邀请展、林兆华戏剧邀请展、北京青年戏剧节、乌镇戏剧节、南锣鼓巷戏剧节等国内戏剧节、邀请展成为了解国际戏剧的窗口和对接国际戏剧市场的平台，并在引进剧目上逐步形成了各自的定位，引进剧目类型多样、层次丰富。

既有外国名导名团名作，如波兰导演陆帕的《英雄广场》、德国导演奥斯特玛雅的《理查三世》、英国皇家莎士比亚剧团的"亨利五世三部曲"等作品；也有小体量、带有实验性的剧目，如法国作品《爱的落幕》、立陶宛作品《三姐妹》《马达加斯加》等。此外，创意舞台秀也成为备受欢迎的艺术形式，2016年美国的《蓝人秀》、加拿大的《大都会》、英国的《破铜烂铁》等演出都登陆中国。

（2）戏曲

2016年专业剧场戏曲演出场次1.52万场，基本与2016年持平，票房收入 8.64 亿元,较 2015 年下降 3.36%(见表 2-4)。戏曲观众人数的减少是戏曲市场规模缩减的主要原因。

表 2-4 2015~2016 年戏曲演出市场对比情况

类别	2015 年	2016 年	增长率(%)
场次(万场)	1.52	1.5153	-0.31
平均票价(元)	200	300	↑
上座率(%)	74	70	↓
观众人数(万人)	342.43	319.20	-6.78
票房收入(亿元)	8.94	8.64	-3.36

专业剧场戏曲演出两极分化。京剧、越剧、豫剧、昆曲等是拥有较广泛受众群的剧种,在政府政策的扶持下,剧目创作、演出场次、保护传统、观众培养等方面都呈现出积极发展的趋势。例如,上海昆剧团的《临川四梦》2016 年巡演 44 场,在广州大剧院连演 4 场,上座率超过九成,总票房达到百万;绍兴大剧院制作的《钗头凤》和《梁山伯与祝英台》2016 年在全国 46 个城市巡演 82 场,上座率超过八成。

传播营销方式的创新为戏曲培育观众、拓宽市场:策划时尚主题吸引年轻观众群,如"十二星座"与京剧传统折子戏搭在一起的主题展演;借助现代金融营销手段,戏迷众筹发起演出,如"王珮瑜京剧清音会——2016 南京站"众筹项目获 302 人次的支持和 85038 元众筹款项;利用现代科技手段推广戏曲的,如小剧场京剧《春日宴》进行了 VR 拍摄,向观众展示时带来如同现场观看的感受。

但大多数地方戏小剧种面临存亡危机,缺少经费、人才断层、市场萎缩、观众流失是大多数地方小剧种的生存现状。

农村市场成为戏曲演出的沃土。受生活风俗和文化消费习惯的影响，戏曲演出在农村有着广阔的市场，近年农村戏曲市场呈现上升发展的良好态势。仅浙江省每年农村戏曲演出就超过21万场，观众达1.5万人次；山西省原平市下辖的520个村，超过65%的农村每年至少要唱7台戏；广东湛江吴川市下辖的1529个自然村，年演出场次达3000多场，票房收入2500多万元，观众近500万人次。

农村戏曲市场的繁荣，一方面得益于农村经济发展，文化消费能力提高，逢年过节、婚丧嫁娶搭台唱戏传统延续发展；另一方面政策鼓励文艺表演团体"送戏下乡"，丰富农村的精神文化生活。

民营文艺表演团体是活跃农村市场的主要力量。例如，浙江嵊州群艺越剧团2016年演出近600场，演出收入达630多万元；湖北省黄冈市黄梅县近百个民营黄梅戏剧团每年在农村演出场次近万场。

伴随着农村戏曲演出市场的发展，演出中介、演出器材制造、演出服饰生产、农村戏台搭建、演出策划宣传、演艺培训等相关行业也发展起来，农村戏曲演出市场的产业链逐渐形成。

（3）儿童剧

2016年专业剧场儿童剧演出场次2.06万场，较2015年上升10.16%，票房收入9.66亿元，较2015年上升7.81%（见表2-5）。

表2-5　2015~2016年儿童剧演出市场对比情况

类别	2015年	2016年	增长率（%）
场次（万场）	1.87	2.06	10.16
平均票价（元）	250	300	↑
上座率（%）	40	50	↑
观众人数（万人）	224.03	255.50	14.05
票房收入（亿元）	8.96	9.66	7.81

儿童剧市场需求旺盛。2016 年儿童剧的观众人数达 255.5 万人，较 2015 年增长了 14.05%，家长对孩子艺术培养的重视、对戏剧教育作用认识的提高等，都是儿童剧市场观众人数提升的原因。儿童剧演出形式更加多样化，例如，上海儿童艺术剧场 2016 年的 40 台 220 多场演出包括了戏剧、音乐、舞蹈、多元四大门类，其中就有现代舞、手影剧、音乐剧等剧目。

可以预测，随着中国生育政策的调整，儿童剧市场的需求将进一步扩大，适合家长和孩子一同观看的家庭演出或将成为市场宠儿。

引进儿童剧目增长，中外儿童剧创作理念差异凸显。2015 年之前，中国演出市场引进儿童剧目十分少见。近两年，引进儿童剧目数量增长、类型多样，例如，2016 年小不点大视界亲子微剧引进了 15 部国外儿童剧，共演出 380 场次，包括英国的亲子环球热舞派对《跳舞吧！宝贝》、西班牙多媒体动画互动剧《猫飞狗跳》、法国装置动画音乐剧《水孩子》等。近距离、互动性、重体验、打破传统观演关系是引进的儿童剧目的突出特点：不一定要通过表演向孩子讲述一个故事、灌输一些道理，而是要更加注重培养儿童的动手能力、社交能力，释放儿童的天性、发掘他们的潜力。

中国儿童剧创作近年也多有创新，比如融入多媒体、3D、虚拟人物等多种技术手段进行表现，但内容上仍没有大的创新，优质原创儿童剧本的缺乏成为制约中国儿童剧发展的重要原因。

4. 曲艺杂技类演出

2016 年专业剧场曲艺杂技类演出场次 0.87 万场，基本与 2015 年持平，票房收入 9.28 亿元，较 2015 年略有提升（见表 2-6）。

表 2-6　2015~2016 年曲艺杂技类演出市场对比情况

类别	2015 年	2016 年	增长率（%）
场次（万场）	0.87	0.8690	-0.11
平均票价（元）	195	210	↑
上座率（%）	41	40	↓
观众人数（万人）	126.62	121.80	-3.81
票房收入（亿元）	9.16	9.28	1.31

（1）曲艺创新开拓市场

既有将现代内容通过传统曲艺形式进行演绎的，例如将流行漫画、网络小说改编为评书吸引年轻观众；也有通过创新营销模式赋予传统曲艺新活力的，例如，上海评弹团通过众筹、推出金融产品、创造卡通周边产品等方式进行商业运作；还有通过互联网平台拓展新空间的，本山传媒、德云社、嘻哈包袱铺等均在多个网络平台进行直播演出。

（2）杂技发展遭遇瓶颈

中国杂技的国内市场一直发展平缓，在国际市场颇受青睐，但近年随着国际市场的饱和，面对恶意降价、无序竞争的市场环境，中国的杂技团生存压力越来越大。中国杂技创作存在重技术技巧、轻艺术表达的问题，缺少故事性、趣味性、创新性，高难度"炫技"的表演形式已无法满足现代观众的观演需求。中国杂技人才培养方式的传统、落后，以及杂技演员培养同样存在重技术技巧培养，轻文化艺术培养的情况，是导致杂技无法突破发展瓶颈的主要原因。此外，训练艰苦、从业周期短、收入水平不高都是造成杂技人才流失、断档的原因，中国杂技编创表演人才培养模式亟待创新。

5. 旅游演出、娱乐演出

（1）旅游演出

2016 年旅游演出场次为 5.29 万场，较 2015 年下降了 4.08%，票房收入 34.04 亿元，较 2015 年下降 3.21%。经过前两年的政策调整期，旅游演出市场下降幅度减缓。

品牌项目稳步增长。以宋城系列、山水系列、印象系列为代表的旅游演出项目稳步增长，2016 年收入增长超过 10%。以宋城演艺项目为例，数据显示，其 2016 年营业收入和净利润增速均超过两位数。

旅游演出品牌项目演出收入逆势上涨，这是从项目选址、投资把控、演艺创意、创作设计、舞台呈现、服装道具、景区运营等各个环节上科学决策、合理把控的结果，这些品牌项目也因此具有更长的生命周期和更好的业绩表现。

演出内容吸引力不足，观众转化率低。根据国家旅游局公布的《中国旅游发展报告（2016）》，2015 年全年国内游客已达 40 亿人次，实现国内旅游业收入 3.42 万亿元，与旅游市场游客人数和旅游收入逐年增长不同，旅游演出观众人数和票房收入连年下降。

中国旅游市场的观众转化率（观众转化率＝全市旅游演出观众数／全市游客数）处于较低水平，绝大多数城市的观众转化率不足 4%（美国纽约的观众转化率为 23%）。即使在观众转化率超过 20% 的丽江，旅游演出市场的情况也不容乐观，丽江旅游局发布的 2016 年年报数据显示，《印象·丽江》全年共演出 750 场，销售门票 154.28 万张，同比下降 23.64%；实现营业收入 1.66 亿元，同比下降 24.48%。

《印象·丽江》就是一个典型案例。其团客占比过高，随着丽江自由行游客迅速增长，旅行团占比下降，拉低了《印象·丽江》的票房收入增速，同时竞争的存在也分流了旅行社的订单。在同一目的地容量有限的情况下，面临同一性质或同个消费类型、消费群体的数个演艺节目之间相互竞争时，常会出现生命周期衰落的情况。文化演出本身也存在喜新厌旧的特点，导致旧有的演艺项目在新项目出现后常常面临较大的竞争压力。旅游演出市场持续下降和观众转化率低的主要原因是旅游演出内容存在剧情单一、故事老套、缺少新鲜感、创新不足、雷同相似、吸引力不足的问题，其中许多项目还有缺乏前期规划和市场评估、盲目跟风和粗制滥造的情况。

（2）演艺场馆娱乐演出

2016 年演艺场馆娱乐演出 48.55 万场，较 2015 年增长 2.04%，票房收入 24.55 亿元，较 2015 年增长 1.99%。

（三）演艺院团与剧场经营优化

2016 年全国文艺表演团体总收入 207.05 亿元，比 2015 年 196.11 亿元，上升 5.58%（见表 2-7）。

表 2-7 2015~2016 年中国演艺院团收入来源构成比较

单位：亿元，%

类别	2015 年	2016 年	增长率
政府补贴	52.88	61.00	15.36
企业赞助	2.50	2.27	−9.20
商业演出	137.04	139.96	2.13
惠民演出	3.69	3.82	3.52
总收入	196.11	207.05	5.58

2016 年，专业剧场演出总场次 8.79 万场，比 2015 年上升 4.52%，总收入 149.05 亿元，比 2015 年上升 1.91%（见表 2-8）。

表 2-8　2015~2016 年中国专业剧场收入来源构成比较

单位：亿元，%

类别	2015 年	2016 年	增长率
场租收入	42.12	40.06	-4.89
自营收入	31.17	34.18	9.66
物业及其他收入	19.96	18.41	-7.77
政府补贴	53.00	56.40	6.41
总收入	146.25	149.05	1.91

1. 院团现代化管理制度逐步建立

文艺表演团体近年来不断深化内部改革，通过现代化技术的运用提升管理水平、完善培养激励机制强化人才支撑、现代化管理制度的建立进一步推动文艺表演团体向真正市场主体转变，从而提高了其创作能力和市场竞争力。

例如北京京剧院采用"合伙人制"，剧院作为出品单位，只支付前期宣传、剧目制作及演出场租等费用，主创人员把创作费、排练费按技术等级与贡献程度入股并参与票房收入分成，提高创作团队的积极性和责任感。

在人才管理方面，上海歌舞团实施"艺衔"制度。形成了首席、独舞 A、独舞 B、领舞 A、领舞 B 和群舞 6 个"艺衔"等次，既确保了拔尖人才的培养优势和引领效应，又夯实了骨干人才队伍基础，形成了结构合理的舞蹈人才梯队。上海芭蕾舞团（简称上芭）实施的是"双轨制"，一方面把国外优秀人才请进门担当驻团编导、教员、客席演员，打造上芭出品的优质剧目；另一方面，积极将本团明星舞者送到国际一流芭蕾舞团进行交流，让他们在互相切磋中锤炼、成长，这样的制度使上芭人才结构更趋合理。

很多文艺表演团体还通过电子化手段，为史料建立数字艺术档案，使珍贵的资料能够更久远地保存，也为艺术档案的推广、普及发挥更大的作用。

2. 剧场自营演出增加，业态优化

2016 年专业剧场自营演出的场次和收入都较 2015 年上升，出租场地演出的场次和收入较 2015 年均下降（见表 2-9）。自营演出场次的比例从 2015 年的 42.57% 提升为 2016 年的 48.35%，自营演出比例的提高说明剧场管理逐步摆脱出租场地的低水平管理模式，许多剧场通过策划演出季、打造品牌剧目展、参与剧目创作等方式优化剧场业态结构，提升演出运营水平，形成了自己的经营特色和演出品牌。例如，天津大剧院举办的天津曹禺国际戏剧节以汇集国内外高水准的戏剧演出备受关注；以"音乐剧专业剧场"为定位的上海文化广场 2016 年试水音乐剧整剧制作，打造了自制音乐剧《春之觉醒》。

表 2-9　2015~2016 年专业剧场演出场次、收入对比情况

类别	场次（万场）		增长率（%）	收入（亿元）		增长率（%）
	2015 年	2016 年		2015 年	2016 年	
出租场地演出场次	4.83	4.54	-6.00	42.12	40.06	-4.89
自营演出场次	3.58	4.25	18.72	31.17	34.18	9.66

（四）演出经纪机构活跃

2016 年全国演出经纪机构总收入 141.76 亿元，比 2015 年 133.07 亿元，上升 6.53%。2016 年演艺经纪机构收入构成情况见图 2-5。

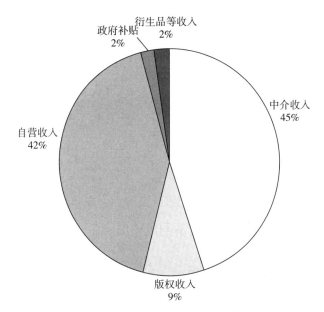

图 2-5　2016 年演艺经纪机构收入构成

1. 以 IP 为核心的版权运营收入增长，泛娱乐化布局初现

演出经纪机构版权收入逐年递增，2016 年为 13.29 亿元，较 2015 年增长 6.41%。演出版权价值逐步被开发，不断增值，内容 IP 被资本看好，一些传统演出经纪机构依托 IP 开始深度布局，例如，话剧《李雷和韩梅梅》《滚蛋吧，肿瘤君》《栀子花开》等作品的出品方——北京世纪华鹏文化传媒有限公司以舞台剧的孵化和开发为先导，在文旅演艺、戏影联动领域深度布局；北京开心麻花娱乐文化传媒股份有限

公司围绕喜剧元素开发多样的产品，进一步提升开心麻花话剧、音乐剧、儿童剧在商业演出市场的份额和影响力，将现有的优质 IP 向网络剧、影视剧等产品上改编，逐步完善喜剧人才孵化平台及相关创新业务板块；宋城演艺确立了演艺、旅游、互联网演艺、艺人 IP 孵化、VR 主题公园及海外项目的泛娱乐布局目标。

2. 小众艺人演出项目系列化"捆绑"运营

小众艺人市场号召力不足，独立市场运营能力有限，一些经纪机构通过整合小众艺人资源，提供专业经纪团队，策划演出项目，进行商业运作。例如，聚橙网打造的"万有音乐系"就是以打造中小型流行音乐现场为方向，2016 年在其品牌下运作了 40 组艺人的演出，其中包括好妹妹乐队、陈粒、马頔等有一定知名度的歌手；大麦也启动"Mailive 一人一巡"音乐计划，以千人级别的剧院作为首选场馆，集合汪苏泷、徐良、李炜等 20 组不同风格的音乐人带来演出。

（五）政府扶持方式转变

政府对演艺市场的扶持方式进一步转变，扶持方式由原来的直接财政拨款向基金资助、补贴票价、政府购买服务等转变，扶持目的由原来的财政供养向激发市场主体活力、培育观众、补齐短板、协调配置资源等转变，扶持对象由原来的仅面向国有单位向兼顾民营单位转变，扶持机制由原来的"花钱不问效"向引入公开招标、评定审议、绩效考核等转变。除国家艺术基金外，江苏、北京等地设立了省级艺术基金，对艺术发展发挥引导和激励作用。演艺产业的发展受到国家层面的政策重视与支持，文化部在《"十三五"时期文化发展改革规划》中，将"重点推出 50 部左右体现时代文化成就、代表国家文化形象的舞台艺术优秀作品。实现名家传戏 1000 人次，扶持 100 部舞台艺术剧本创作"作为"十三五"期间文化发展主要指标的重要内容。

在政府购买服务方面,文化部出台了《文化部向社会力量购买服务管理方法》和相应的指导性目录,将公益性演出纳入政府采购范围,国有院团特别是转制院团将来可参与采购招标,通过提供演出服务的方式获得支持。根据文化部、财政部等四部委 2015 年印发的《关于做好政府向社会力量购买公共文化服务工作的意见》的要求,各级政府根据本地区情况因地制宜,出台本地区的购买指导意见,将文艺演出纳入政府购买目录,多地还出台了政府购买公益性文艺演出的工作方案,很多地区形成了"百姓点单、社会接单、政府买单"的机制。例如,上海市 2016 年下半年公共文化配送项目中包括大型演出和中型演出各 800 场;山西省 2016 年财政出资 1100 多万元,购买省八大剧团的公共演出 400 多场,惠及观众 40 多万人次。政府购买文艺演出服务再把符合群众需求的演出送到基层,既丰富了人们的精神文化生活,又发挥了培育市场的作用。

低票价补贴政策直接惠及观众,有利于培养演出消费习惯,吸引更多人走进剧院。以天津为例,天津市文化广播影视局、市财政局制定出台了《支持高雅演出、精品展览和公益文化普及活动专项经费管理暂行办法》,对天津大剧院引进的高端演出给予补贴;天津推出适用于 11 家市级国有院团演出的"文惠卡",市民只需支付 100 元即可领取一张面值 500 元的文惠卡,政府补贴 400 元,观看演出还可享受三到八折优惠。

值得关注的是,在引导文艺创作,培育演出市场方面,北京多措并举,形成了前端艺术基金扶持创作、中端剧目排练中心提供保障、末端剧院服务平台对接供需、终端低票价惠及广大观众的涉及全产业链的政策格局。

（六）演艺与互联网双向融合

互联网与演艺在加速融合发展，"互联网＋"为演艺产业带来了传播方式、营销方式、盈利方式、体验方式等诸多改变，演艺也为互联网平台提供了内容、带来了用户。在线直播已经成为演唱会的必选项，在带来版权、网络票房等收益的同时，受众数百倍的增长也提升了演出潜在的商业价值。例如，李宇春"野蛮生长"巡回演唱会北京站在乐视的直播，同步观看的人数超过 566 万，而 2014 年汪峰演唱会的数据是 4.8 万；备受关注的王菲"幻乐一场"上海演唱会在腾讯的直播最高峰在线观看人数突破了 2100 万。此外，随着 VR 等技术的普及应用，互联网将为观众带来新的观演体验。

互联网平台也不满足于仅作网络转播方，纷纷布局线下。例如，乐视音乐参与主办了 MTA 天漠音乐节和李宇春 2016 年巡回演唱会；票务平台格瓦拉与十三月文化公司合资成立公司，为艺人唱片、优质巡演提供全方位的运营服务。

演艺领域也在不断开拓线上业务。例如，上海交响乐团打造"在线数字音乐厅"，加大对大型音乐场馆直播云平台的研发和应用，建立音乐会播出平台；导演赖声川推出网络情景喜剧《王子富愁记》，在剧场实景搭建拍摄，开启生活同步编剧，将现场观众的互动以及征集到的线上观众的意见融入剧本创作中。

（七）资本逐渐涌入演艺市场

虽然目前中国国内演艺产业整体规模较小，演艺院团、机构规模小，相比其他行业演艺投融资仍然存在较高的风险，但在中国演艺市场不断成熟和完善的过程中，演艺投融资逐渐可以进行评估，具备可控性——观演逐渐成为人们的一种生活方式，演出宣传与营销渠道已依托大城市形成网络并开始辐射全国，产业结构不断优化，演艺产业链分工也越来越细，产业融合加速，带动作用明显。这些都将推动中国演艺市场的投融资变得更有目的性和方向性，投资收益情况更加有据可依，投资回报率也将随之上升。演艺版权交易，互动、开放和融合的新型票务平台，服务大型演出的数字化舞美机构，演艺网络平台，演艺产品和服务的新兴营销平台等一系列演艺市场新的增长点都有望成为投资热宠。诸如游客规模大、具有强有力营销渠道的旅游演出，拥有全国巡演渠道和忠实观众群体的商业剧目，观众认知度较高的国际经典引进剧目，具有消费号召力的跨界演艺品牌（如动漫、卡通改编的儿童剧），集演出、培训、娱乐于一体的综合开发项目等优质的演艺相关项目也将吸引投资者的目光。

1. 资本入驻演艺市场相对缓慢

2014年3月17日文化部、中国人民银行、财政部联合发布了《关于深入推进文化金融合作的意见》，强调了文化金融合作的重要意义和发展机遇，鼓励创新文化金融体制机制、创新符合文化产业发展需求特点的金融产品与服务，为文化金融合作的顺利开展提供配套保障。

2014年下半年云南杨丽萍文化传播股份有限公司完成新三板挂牌，标志着中国正式开启演艺资本之路，国内演艺机构开始加速与资本市场合作的步伐。据不完全统计，自2015年起杭州金海岸文化发展股份有限公司、北京开心麻花娱乐文化传媒股份有限公司、山东世博演艺股份有限公司、厦门市天视文化传媒股份有限公司、北京锋尚世纪文化传媒股份有限公司、河南百禾传媒有限公司、杭州新青年歌舞团股份有限公司等十多家演艺机构结合各自特点通过资本运作的方式成功在新三板挂牌。2017年3月中国电子商务公司阿里巴巴全资收购了国内最大的在线票务平台大麦网，将其纳入阿里巴巴大文娱战略板块……资本也在寻找适合的对象进行投资，例如，华人文化控股集团和华人文化产业投资基金联手入股运营大型女子偶像团体"SNH48"的丝芭传媒；聚橙网获得了海通开元领投，建发新兴投资、九弦资本、温氏投资等机构跟投的数亿元pre-ipo轮融资；商业舞台剧团"至乐汇"获得了和（上海）影业有限公司领投的数千万元人民币的天使轮融资。演艺虽一直受资本关注，但相比其他文化行业演艺基本是资本入驻最晚的文化行业领域，就资本市场而言，演出机构由于运营内容类型较单一，受非市场因素影响多，易受单个作品市场效果反馈影响等特点，并不具有太多优势，因而资本介入演艺市场也相对谨慎。

2. 二级票务平台受资本青睐

近两年，多个二级票务平台相继建立，二级票务市场被资本看好（见表2-10）。二级票务市场作为一级票务市场的补充，发挥着市场调剂的作用，有其存在的必要和发展的空间。但由于一些平台运营不规范、管理有漏洞、监管手段不完善，成为黄牛票甚至是假票的集散地，对溢价票干预机制的缺失，又成为个别人牟取暴利的途径，扰乱了演出市场秩序，侵害了消费者权益。政府主管部门应对这一新业态出台管理办法，加强规范和监管。

3. 演出资金来源逐步成熟，众筹成为新兴亮点

因为对演艺业前景的看好，演出行业的投资机制越来越成熟完善，更多微小的演艺企业走上了精良制作的道路，而大型的文化企业也不断拓展自己的发展空间。其中，众筹的方式近年来尤为突出，逐渐成为一种趋势，一方面让高端的演出走进了人们的生活，不再遥不

表 2-10　部分二级票务平台运营模式及融资情况

平台	模式	成立时间	融资金额	融资时间
西十区	B2B2C C2B2C	2011 年底	Pre-A 轮投资数百万元	2013 年 1 月
			A 轮 3000 万元融资	2014 年 10 月
			A+ 轮 5000 万元	2016 年 1 月
牛魔王	B2B2C	2015 年 7 月	A 轮数百万美元	2016 年 10 月
			A+ 轮千万美元	2016 年 11 月
一号票仓	B2B	2015 年 12 月	天使轮数千万元	2016 年 6 月
有票网	C2C	2016 年	天使轮 500 万元	2016 年 6 月

资料来源：中国演出行业协会《2016 年中国演出市场年度报告》。

可及；另一方面也让小众高质的演出节目得到了生存和提高知名度的方法。

以 2016 年广受关注的众筹京剧《龙凤呈祥》为例，这一众筹项目利用年轻一代对互联网理财的兴趣，将文化产品的收益与投资者的收益结合，传统戏曲与互联网众筹碰撞融合，以一种新颖的形式宣告了传统文化艺术的华丽回归，传统文化被更多的人所关注和熟知，文化众筹成为传统文化寻求新的表达方式的着力点。需要注意的是，尽管文化众筹在发展演艺产业、提升文化产业的生命力上具有很大的作用，但大多数的文化产品，特别是传统的文化产品，在经过了互联网的简单加工之后，仍然不具备非常强的竞争优势，依然面临着发展困境，所以应该继续深入探求演艺业与众筹之间的结合路径，以及更加丰富优质的资金来源。

中国正在逐步进入文化娱乐消费较快增长的阶段，人们观演休闲娱乐需求趋势日渐明显，与国际成熟演艺市场和中国国内电影市场做对比，演艺市场发展潜力还未释放。可以预见，演艺将获得越来越多资本的关注，越来越多的演出机构也有意借力资本，寻求新发展。

（八）中国演艺市场整合速度加快

1. 主体业务多元拓展

越来越多的演出市场主体开始立足主营优势业务，向产业链上下游进行多元拓展，建立自身内部产业生态格局。

国有演艺机构中有剧场院线管理公司开始对下属的演出公司进行改组，将其业务由以演出经纪为主转型为以原创制作为主；搭建票务营销平台，了解会员需求，调整上游业务服务，逐步由单一的靠剧院管理、票房收入盈利向票务代理、演出组织、版权交易、线上剧院等多点盈利发展。有的民营演出单位则形成了以演出经纪为主体，演出制作、演出票务、剧院运营并行的"1+3"完整产业链，其中演出经纪的运营主体为母公司，剧目制作、剧院管理、票务业务则分别由三家子公司承担。而演出票务网站如大麦网则冠名大连体育中心体育馆，进军线下场馆运营领域，在重点城市打造智慧场馆，从系统、内容到信息化三方面帮助场馆有效提升商业价值和合作空间。

一些传统演出机构也开始泛娱乐布局，例如，永乐文化从单纯的票务公司发展为综合性的文化娱乐企业，目前已拥有票务、影业、演艺、科技、体育、经纪、二次元、公关等多个泛娱乐业务板块；宋城演艺确立了演艺、旅游、互联网演艺、艺人 IP 孵化、VR 主题公园及海外项目的泛娱乐布局目标。

2. 演艺市场跨界融合凸显

2014 年 2 月 26 日，国务院印发《关于推进文化创意和设计服务与相关产业融合发展的若干意见》（国发〔2014〕10 号），为实现"提升旅游发展文化内涵"的重点任务，在意见中提出"支持开发具有地域特色和民族风情的旅游演艺精品和旅游商品"。文化产业融合发展步伐加快，演艺业与影视、旅游等文化产业核心及相关行业的融合为中国演艺市场带来了新的活力，开拓了更广阔的市场空间。

旅游演艺在全国演艺市场中一直占有相当比例。受 2013 年 10 月出台的《旅游法》对旅游演出市场的持续影响，2014 年旅游演出市场继续呈较大幅度下降趋势。旅游演出市场受政策规范影响的下降会持续较长时间，主要原因在于，除少数品牌性项目之外，大部分旅游演出项目制作水平普遍偏低，缺乏创意，缺乏市场吸引力，取消旅行社捆绑消费方式后这些项目难以为继。但这并不影响旅游与演艺融合的趋势，2015 年全国旅游演出观众 4713 万人次，较 2014 年增长 31.2%；2015 年全年在演剧目 195 台，较 2014 年减少 28 台；2015 年旅游演出实收票房达 35.7 亿元，较 2014 年增长 31.7%。

二 2016 年中国演艺市场对外贸易特点

近年来，在全球文化产业和服务贸易发展的宏观背景下，国际演出市场竞争要素流动性加速，跨国演出活动和剧目版权贸易日趋频繁。在政府利好产业政策、行业规范和配套服务平台不断健全的影响下，依托演艺市场的持续繁荣，演艺对外贸易在剧目数量、巡演场次、观演人次及演出贸易额等方面继续呈现稳步增长的态势。2016 年演艺对外贸易在创作、主体发展、发展支持政策、平台建设等各方面保持着积极的发展态势。

（一）各地演艺市场联系日益紧密

2016 年以一线城市演艺市场为核心，借由优秀剧目的巡演，各地演艺市场向着更加联通、更加完整的全国性演艺市场发展。对外贸易的基础是国内市场的高度繁荣，国内演艺市场的高度发展才能催生出高质量的演出剧目，利用国内市场演艺收入摊平演艺产品与服务开拓海外市场的成本，使其在国际演艺市场更具竞争力。一线演艺团体不断拓展演出范围，有利于演艺市场相对成熟的大城市优秀的文化资源和院团运作模式向演艺市场仍在起步、发展阶段的二三线城市传播，有助于缩短不同地区演艺市场与演艺主体发展的差距，使得全国向着统一的文化市场发展，从而提升全国的演艺业水平，进一步为全国演艺产品与服务的出口打下产业基础。

国内演艺市场是发展演艺对外贸易的前提和基础，国内演艺市场催生高品质的演艺产品与服务，创造了旺盛的演艺消费需求，同时也意味着人们对本国文化的高度认同和深刻理解，是表达文化自信，实现跨文化、跨时代沟通的体现。随着"一带一路"沿线国家发展各自的文化产业、文化市场，中国消费者的演艺消费需求也将逐步外溢到"一带一路"沿线国家的演艺产品与服务，国内演艺市场的产品与服务也将吸引"一带一路"沿线国家的演艺消费需求。

（二）演艺进口助推演艺出口

2016 年演艺市场对外贸易依然以剧目引进为主，但引进剧目直接原版搬上舞台的模式也逐渐开始发生改变，越来越多的院团和演艺企业将引进剧目进行了本土化改编，逐渐参与制作发行甚至对剧目进行创作改编。一方面使其更加适应国内观众的观演偏好，另一方面对剧目的改编也是解构剧目，学习国外成熟剧目创作、排演成功经验的有效办法，因而不仅可以更好地把握市场需求，更能推动演艺院团自身原创剧目的发展。

国内院团开始更加注重中外合作制作的模式，从引进剧目，到联合制作出品，再到宣传营销，国外团队在合作中为国内院团注入了大量新鲜的血液，从而更加有利于国内院团在创作和演出方面更具市场化、国际化的思维。以中国国家话剧院与英国国家剧院合作出品的《战马》为例，其中文版在国家话剧院演出了 58 场，吸引观众超过五万人次，平均上座率达到 95%，称得上是一部现象级大剧，从而成为万众瞩目的文化热点。《战马》中文版在制作中学习借鉴了英国国家话剧院的经验，比如在演员选拔方面，中国国家话剧院就首次采用了社会公开招聘的形式，这一模式不仅有利于寻找更多的优秀人才，而且无形中为《战马》进行前期的大规模宣传。虽然《战马》的投入很高，但它的票价是十分亲民的，仅为普通同类演出的 1/3 左右，战马票务公司专门用于为《战马》中文版进行专属票务服务，改变了以往国内大制作舞台剧票价曲高和寡的局面。在学习和创新中，中方慢慢地对引进的剧目进行消化吸收变成自己的东西，中国国际演出剧院联盟已经承包了《战马》亚洲演出的独家运营权，并且借鉴英国首次实行"全产业链"的营销模式。近期，中方《战马》团队还与韩国共同合作，制作《战马》的韩文版，从而实现从"引进来"到"走出去"的华丽转身。

（三）演艺出口贸易增长

1. 出口额增长

2016 年文艺表演团体赴海外演出收入为 17.14 亿元，较 2015 年提高了 4.42%。

"走出去"的演出不仅有中国在国际市场较有竞争力的杂技项目，例如，湖南省杂技艺术剧院的大型原创杂技剧《梦之旅》在美国、加拿大的 70 多个城市演出 100 场，观众达 20 多万人次；也有交响乐、芭蕾舞等源于西方的艺术形式，例如，上海芭蕾舞团的豪华版《天鹅湖》2016 年完成了在荷兰的 26 场巡演、《葛蓓莉娅》在加拿大蒙特利尔的 5 场演出、《简·爱》在波兰彼得哥什的两场演出、《长恨歌》在英国伦敦的 5 场演出以及古典芭蕾舞剧《吉赛尔》与四幕原创芭蕾舞剧《梁山伯与祝英台》在加拿大渥太华的演出。此外，中国传统戏曲艺术也在拓展国际市场中取得了一定成绩，例如，浙江小百花越剧团创排的《寇流兰与杜丽娘》在英国、法国、德国、奥地利进行了为期 22 天的巡演。

演艺院团通过政府资助和商业运作的方式"走出去"，一方面传播中国文化，扩大中国文化的国际影响力；另一方面开拓国际市场，了解国际市场的运作规律，与海外机构建立合作关系，提高商业运作能力，逐步变"走出去"为"卖出去"。

2. 出口以剧目输出贸易为主导

国家文化部外联局数据显示，全国以杂技为主的民族演艺产品的对外演出创汇额比重达 80%。中国演艺出口目前依旧以杂技、功夫剧和民族舞台剧为主，国际演出市场主流的音乐剧和歌舞剧演出则显得较为缺乏，而且杂技和功夫剧的海外市场逐渐萎缩。中国杂技团体在海外市场繁杂，一味追求短期演出收益，长期将单个剧目订单式地出售给海外杂技院团，甚至直接将杂技演员以劳务输出的形式签至海外杂技院团名下，不仅失去了剧目版权和衍生产品收入，更没有树立自己的杂技品牌，缺乏具有影响力的剧目，院团彼此之间存在恶性竞争，加之国际经济形势致使杂技、功夫剧的海外订单锐减。

同时，中国演艺院团、企业对外演出中依旧以单纯的剧目贸易为主，演出版权贸易的比重依旧较低。剧目输出贸易的形式使得国内演出公司除了获得演出合同所议定的收益外,无法分享更多的演出收益,更重要的是相比版权贸易输出,剧目输出无法在海外市场形成规模演出场次,市场影响力低。并且演艺院团的海外活动基本为单次演出项目业务,与院团、院线联盟相关的对外合作、兼并及收购等业务寥寥无几。

(四)演艺院团自主"走出去"意愿强烈

2016 年,中央与地方演出团体、机构赴国外及中国港澳台地区演出依然十分活跃,民族特色鲜明,艺术形式丰富多彩。随着全国演艺市场的发展,国有、民营院团及其他演出经营主体参与对外演出的积极性不断提高,对外演出服务交易平台不断完善,演出贸易形式从剧目跨境演出的传统单一型向剧目版权贸易、院线联盟代理、中外合资制作等多元化方向过渡发展,更多的演艺院团走出国门,拓展海外演出市场,尽可能地减少对政府扶持政策的依赖,让市场成为院团发展的活力来源,拓展出一条市场化运作道路。例如北京京剧院以"京剧合伙人"的名义推出了小剧场京剧剧目《碾玉观音》,这是一种开放思路的模式,剧院只作为出品单位,主创人员把自己的个人收入作为投资入股该剧目,从而票房直接与创作人员收入挂钩,大大激发了他们的主动性和积极性。在剧目营销方面也尽可能多地使用易被年轻人接受的营销渠道,将观众的年龄层次进一步扩大。

2016 年中国演出市场与国际市场的合作全方位发力,多点开花,以开放的姿态推动深入融合。演出领域国际合作逐步深入,且向版权交易、参股投资等方面拓展。文艺表演团体间的合作不再流于表面,而是有了更多自主和多样的深度合作,包括艺术家培养、互访演出、剧目联合制作、管理模式更新等。例如,北京国际音乐节艺术法国普罗旺斯－埃克斯国际艺术节签订 5 年的合作计划望通过联合制作、联合委约以及合作开展教育项目、公众参与项目等方式进行深度合作；山水盛典文化产业有限公司与越国文化管理演出公司签署越南五地的实景演出协议，共同对越南本土历史、文化进行挖掘、呈现与拓展；上海东方秀剧场投资管理公司参股英国 ATG（大使剧院集团）所属公司排演的音乐剧《红男绿女》全部演出场次；在版权方面，圆核经典文化传媒以版权购买的形式引进加拿大舞台秀《舞马》，并在北京演出 150 场。

相比较发达国家的对外演出贸易，中国演艺产业在对外演出剧目创新、贸易融资和保险、国际演出经纪推介、院线代理营销、贸易法律咨询及贸易规范统计等诸多方面还需不断努力，减小相对贸易差额，提升演出经营主体单位的国际竞争优势。

（五）大型文化交流项目寻求市场转型

随着演艺市场化的发展，文化贸易在文化传播中的作用日益凸显，逐渐与文化交流同样重要，而且文化贸易凭借市场运作带来的经济效益相比主要依靠政府财政支持的文化交流项目更具有可持续性。在国家大力发展文化产业和文化贸易的背景下，依循文化交流模式的演艺院团也在逐渐转变，开始寻求社会资金的参与，推动剧目适应市场化常态。尤其是综合性的文艺晚会等大型文化交流项目开始尝试通过商业合作实现转型。

"欢乐春节"是国家创立的大型综合性文化活动品牌，旨在把春节打造成中华文化"走出去"知名品牌。"欢乐春节"活动至今已经成功举办了五届，集国内和国外、中央和地方、国有和民营等各方资源，是迄今为止在海外举办的规模最大的对外文化工作品牌活动，推出广场巡游、民俗庙会、综艺演出、电视晚会、图书展等形式多样的活动，为中国开展文化外交、文化交流、文化贸易和提升国家软实力等提供了一个重要平台，成为推动中华文化"走出去"的一个亮丽品牌。

"欢乐春节"在发展过程中并没有完全依赖国家财政支持，而是积极在全球范围内寻找合作伙伴。通过采取搭建平台、拓展渠道、资金补贴等有效措施和手段，"欢乐春节"活动曾先后推出百余项高品质的商业性项目，为推动国际文化贸易，增添自身可持续发展力积蓄了巨大潜能。同时随着"欢乐春节"活动影响的不断提升，越来越多的中国文化企业和产品借助"欢乐春节"提供的良好平台与国际市场接轨。由京文唱片公司投资制作的大型中国风情舞台剧《熊猫》于春节期间亮相拉斯维加斯；俏佳人传媒股份有限公司在洛杉矶成功举办"2014 好莱坞中国新年电视晚会"，覆盖现场和电视观众数千万。市场化运作模式让海外"欢乐春节"活动在春节文化的对外传播和院团走向世界两方面实现了双赢——演艺院团的介入为"欢乐春节"活动从形式到内容上注入了新的活力，而"欢乐春节"又为优秀演艺院团提供了走向世界的平台。

（六）海外演艺版权投融资增加

随着中国经济发展的越来越好，以及文化产业越来越热，不仅仅是文化产业领域里的企业，许多其他行业的企业也开始进行文化产业的投融资活动，特别是海外投资。近年来世界萧条的经济状况对于中国海外投资者来说是一个利好的消息，成本和风险相对较低，且能以较小的成本收购和并购一些优秀、品质很好的公司。特别是文化，作为非必需品，在经济发展较为停滞的时期，容易被当作挤出市场泡沫的首要之选。

演艺方面，许多企业逐步开始对海外演艺版权进行投资，包括剧场的收购、剧目IP的买断等。投资一方面走向英国伦敦西区、美国百老汇等的经典成熟剧目，比如聚橙网开始投资购买美国百老汇的音乐剧；另一方面，部分企业不止步于此，想更多地参与剧目的一系列制作流程等，以长远的眼光，投资新创的剧目，在剧目编创前期就进行投入，一直跟踪支持，从而能够更好更完整地把版权引入中国。其中，各大票务公司是活跃在演出市场的力量，他们基于自身平台的数据分析等优势，投资舞台剧、参与开发IP、投资运营剧院等。以永乐票务为例，2015年其投资主办的"林肯公园猎捕行动中国巡回演唱会"开启了欧美摇滚乐队在中国开展万人体育场级规模巡演的先河，获得了口碑和票房的双赢。另外，在韩国等演艺发达国家，永乐票务开始设立分公司，从而能更快地拥有优质的内容资源。

（七）国家级演艺贸易服务平台建立

2014年文化部为建立健全机制，优化公共服务，建立国际文化贸易合作体系，对海内外文化市场进行战略布局，着手搭建了公共服务平台，逐步形成以演艺、数字内容、学术研究、法律援助为核心的服务平台，联合行业协会和研究机构，为文化企业"走出去"提供优质公共服务。

文化部委托中国演出行业协会组建了"演艺产品出口公共服务平台"，有针对性地汇集外向型演艺企业和项目，加强与海外行业协会、交易会和经纪公司的合作，逐步打通中国演艺产品进出口渠道，并以公开、科学的遴选机制对演艺服务出口进行资金扶持，面向全国选拔支持示范项目。具体来说演艺产品出口公共服务平台在信息服务方面，建立涵盖演出创意、制作、营销领域的国内外演艺专家资源库，建立分地域、分类型、带有出口配套信息服务的国内演艺产品资源库，建立涵盖海外演出场所、演出经纪机构、艺术节等的海外需求信息资源库，协助演艺产品出口单位扩大海外合作渠道和范围；在渠道服务方面，提供海外演艺展会和各类艺术节信息，推动国际演艺展会组织落地中国，举办中国演艺产品国际营销年会，为中国演艺产品出口搭建国际推广平台；在人才培养方面，与国际知名艺术院校、剧院、经纪公司合作，增强演出经纪人员文化贸易相关知识培训，组织演艺企业骨干赴海外主要艺术节、演出机构考察学习；在演艺产品宣传推广方面，充分利用驻外使领馆、海外文化中心和海外媒体、新媒体，为优秀外向型演艺产品搭建多方位的宣传推广平台，同时建立相应的网络服务窗口。

文化部委托北京第二外国语学院牵头组建国家文化贸易学术研究平台（简称学术研究平台），由国家文化发展国际战略研究院承担秘书处工作，目前已协同国内外 35 家大学及研究机构，直接服务于成员间沟通、协调与合作以及海内外各项活动的组织举办。学术研究平台现汇聚国内外文化贸易理论实践的力量，基于对国际文化贸易规则的准确把握，助力中国对外贸易结构调整，以学术研究促进海外文化市场有效拓展，推动文化企业参与文化贸易实践，深入挖掘并推广诸多中国对外文化贸易经典案例，培养国家急需的具有中国灵魂、国际视野的高级文化经营管理人才，逐步建设成为服务国家战略的外脑平台、理论与实践的研究平台以及人才培养的联动平台。国家文化贸易学术研究平台作为学术先行者为中国演艺市场的国际化发展提供学术支持、人才保障和研究服务。

此外文化部还委托中国文化产业协会牵头组建"国家数字内容贸易服务平台"，既包括信息交流、论坛会议、参展参奖等传统平台性业务，更进一步结合"互联网+"，建设运营在线平台，利用数字内容产品所具有的高度标准化、数字化、虚拟化特征，以制作贸易为突破口，打破时间、空间、软件、支付的限制，真正实现在线制作远程管理、在线贸易支付、在线信用等级评价等功能，逐步推动版权贸易、投资贸易向前发展，为包括演艺企业在内的文化企业提供数字化支持和互联网平台。

演艺对外贸易相关的国家平台的建立必将覆盖全国演艺市场，使得演艺院团在认识自身优势和不足、获取国际演艺市场动态信息、了解国际演出渠道、聘用和培训艺术表演与经营管理人才等各方面获得巨大助力，演艺对外贸易将更有方向性，更加有组织、有计划，很大程度上避免单独开辟国际市场给院团自身带来过高的额外演出成本。

（八）文化基金推动演艺对外贸易

2014年基金制度开始引入文化市场，使得国家支持包括演艺在内的各文化行业发展的资金得到更加系统、公正、合理的管理和使用，从而增进了国内演艺市场的活力，缓解了演艺对外贸易的资金压力。国家艺术基金成立于2013年12月30日，是国家设立、政府主导、专家评审、面向社会的专业性、公益性基金，资助范围涵盖了戏剧、音乐、舞蹈、曲艺、杂技、木偶、皮影、美术、书法、摄影等十几个大的艺术门类中近80种艺术形式，成为国家管理、资助、扶持和引导艺术事业健康发展的新平台、新渠道、新机制。国家艺术基金的设立对于文化艺术的发展具有重要意义，它是推进国家治理体系和治理能力现代化的具体举措，是推进中国艺术治理"管""办"分离、激发全社会文化创造力的体制机制创新的又一成果。国家艺术基金改变了以往财政投入直接"养人"的模式，通过间接赞助、专家评审、社会监督、绩效考评等手段，充分发挥了财政资金的导向作用，保证资金投入和资金使用的公开、公平、公正、透明，也有利于督促被资助者努力提高资金使用效率。

2016 年共有 6493 个各类机构和个人作为申报主体，向国家艺术基金申报了 7248 个项目，申请资助资金总额 75.1 亿元。与 2015 年度相比，申报项目量增加了 2846 项，增幅 64.7%，较 2014 年度增加约七成。2016 年申报项目中舞台艺术创作 2495 项，占申报总量 34.4%，其中大型舞台剧和作品 1106 项、小型舞台剧（节）目和作品 1389 项，与 2015 年度相比，分别增加了 285 项、600 项，增幅 34.7%、76%；大型舞台剧和作品进入复评 291 项，立项资助 146 项，立项率 13.2%；小型剧（节）目和作品进入复评 429 项，立项资助 159 项，立项率 11.4%。2016 年度舞台艺术创作资助项目不再设立大型舞台剧和作品重大加工修改提高项目，体现了基金资助原创性、源头性、基

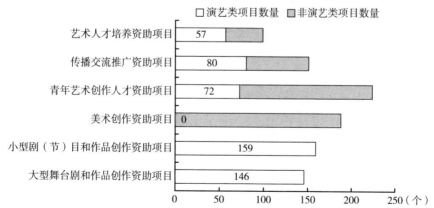

图 2-6　2016 年度国家艺术基金支持各类项目中演艺及相关项目分布

础性项目的原则，以更好地发挥支持新作品创作的"孵化器"作用，创作新作品的积极性得到充分调动。[①]

三　2016 年中国演艺业对外贸易亟待破解的问题

（一）系统的统计评估体系亟待建立

当前，中国文化主管部门和演出行业协会在演出数据和演出贸易统计方面依旧处于非规范的状态，各级政府没有实时的演艺统计制度，行业年度报告统计口径差异较大，凸显了对外演出贸易监管的缺位。中国演出行业协会发布的数据具有较高的准确度，是目前普遍使用的全国演艺业年度数据。但中国演出行业协会的统计指标仅包含演出场次、票房、票价等最主要的基础演艺数据，并没有更系统和细化的指标设计。而且由于全国没有建立统一的统计体系，也没有规定统计标准，因此各省市、地区的演艺数据可比性很低，对跨地区的统计数据分析造成严重阻碍，给演艺市场研究分析的客观性带来局限和干扰。同时对相关演艺支持政策发挥的调控作用、国家资助资金的使用成效、演艺院团演出取得的经济和社会效益等缺乏合理的评估体系，导致演艺政策得不到反馈，也无法通过事后绩效考核的形式发现院团享受政府政策优惠产生的作用以及监管支持资金的用途，不能对院团产生约束。

统计评估体系的缺失使得无论是政府还是演艺院团、演艺行业组织机构都无法较为精确地判断演艺市场规模、剧目类型、观众票房以及社会影响力等，不能对全国演艺市场当前的发展有更全面的认识，

---

① 数据来源：国家艺术基金官网及微信公众账号。

进而影响了其对演艺市场未来走向的预判，这就导致了政府决策没有依据，院团发展把握不准方向。

（二）优秀演艺品牌缺失，院团国际化被动发展

在持续引进国际演艺剧目的大背景下，2016 年依然是演艺贸易逆差的一年，具有国际竞争力的演艺剧目和演艺品牌的缺乏仍是制约演艺对外贸易的关键因素。2016 年全国演艺市场新创剧目众多，其中也不乏诸多票房成功的演出新剧目，产生了一定的品牌效应，但统观全国演艺市场，演艺对于明星效应的依赖性依旧明显，仍然没有具有国际影响力和持久演艺活力的院团或剧目品牌脱颖而出。品牌的树立不仅取决于演艺作品创作这一核心环节，还受管理、宣传推广、营销等诸多环节的影响。运作资金不足、管理失衡、定位不准确都会阻碍演艺品牌的产生。资金不足将无法支撑从创作、排演到宣传、销售的整个产业链条；管理的缺失则会降低剧院的运营效率增大运营风险，甚至导致优秀创作、演艺人才的流失。如果对市场定位不准确，则会难以实现优秀的演出剧目与有观演需求的市场受众有效对接，造成资源的浪费。国际演艺市场长期被欧美国家把持，主要原因就是这些国家已经形成具有国际知名度、影响力的高质量演艺品牌。中国演艺院团、企业建立自己的有持续生命力的演艺品牌是与欧美成熟演艺院团、企业竞争的最直接、最有效的办法。

目前中国演艺院团的国际化主要受引进的海外剧目拉动，即在引进海外剧目过程中通过学习借鉴其成熟的运作经验，侧面推动院团国际化进程，尤其是版权引进的以及进行过本土化改编的剧目使得院团对国际经典剧目的创作、排演、推广营销都有了细致的认识。但是这

种被动的国际化途径相比院团主动参与国际演艺市场竞争显得缓慢而滞后，究其原因还是没有经得住国际市场检验的优秀剧目。

（三）现代企业制度不完善

转制国有演艺院团与民营演艺院团在不同方面都存在着现代企业制度不完善的问题。转制国有演艺院团管理机构臃肿，权责不明，管理效率低下。国有院团通过转企改制虽然剥离行政事业单位建立了企业制度，但由股东大会、董事会、监事会、经理层构成的相互依赖又相互制衡的文化企业内部法人结构还不完善，院团领导体制上权利不明、责任不清，要么"一元化"领导缺少监督制约，要么互相扯皮摩擦内耗过大。国有演艺院团转制后大部分的投资主体依然是国家，产权非常单一且产权不清，目前许多转制国有演艺院团本质上还是"事业编制、企业管理"模式，计划经济时代国有企业的种种弊端在当前各转制国有演艺院团中依然严重存在。转制国有演艺院团经营管理人员多为专业的艺术工作者，专业的企业运营知识相对匮乏，管理相对随意，不能与企业的法人治理结构相适应；同时也存在人才选拔不以市场为导向的情况。转制国有演艺院团依然主要依靠国家投资，一些转制国有文化经营单位专门招聘的人员直接被借调至相关政府部门工作，造成了额外的人力资源成本。

民营演艺院团规模小，难以形成规范的法人治理结构。当前许多民营演艺院团处于发展初期，属于中小甚至小微企业，由于股权单一、企业规模小、产品单一、管理简单等原因，实行的都是投资者与经营者两者合一的管理体制，由投资者直接经营管理企业，还没有将企业的所有权与经营权实行分离的需要，也不具备相应条件，很难建立起成熟而系统的法人治理结构。

（四）外向型演艺经营管理人才仍然匮乏

2015 年演艺从业人员规模达到 348612 人（其中艺术表演团体从业人员 301878 人，艺术表演剧场从业人员 46734 人），五年间演艺从业人员规模扩大了近 37.75%。中国不乏一批国家顶级艺术院团和国内外知名的表演艺术家、世界级文化经纪公司等，亦拥有培养国际人才的高等学府，然而面对众多优秀的演艺人员和高质量的教育资源，演艺业的发展依然缺乏大量创作人才和经营管理人才。演艺创作人才的缺乏主要是由于合理的鼓励机制和版权保护机制的缺失，而演艺经营管理人才尤其是外向型经营管理人才更是演艺业人才培养的空白。

在人才培养方面，相比伦敦、纽约等著名的国际化演艺大都市，中国演艺人才的培养与演艺市场的应用与实践严重脱节，高校对于演艺经营管理人才的培养或者只关注演艺作品的生产环节，或者只局限于演艺产品的推广营销，更多的则是拘泥于理论研究层面，从而缺少对于整个演艺业发展现状的清晰认识以及对整个产业链全局的把握，不能及时对演艺市场的需求做出反应与调整，从而无法实现人才供需的有效对接。应用型、复合型、外向型经营管理人才的培养越发急迫。

（五）演艺行业融资环境不完善

为契合 2014 年文化部、中国人民银行、财政部联合发布的《关于深入推进文化金融合作的意见》，政府部门和银行方面实行了一系列的措施，有效地发挥了财政资金的撬动放大作用，促使文化企业在文化产业项目实施过程中能运用更多的金融工具，提升自身市场化融资能力。截至 2015 年 12 月底，中国文化、体育和娱乐业人民币中长期贷款余额 2458 亿元，同比增长 25.7%。[①] 然而，政府的支持依然还无法完全满足所有的文化企业，包括演艺行业企业。

目前演艺产业，尤其是中小企业融资，由于内外各方面的原因，渠道并不畅通。首先是因为演艺产业其本身的特性：投入高、营利模式不稳定、不可控因素多、不能像简单工业一样进行快速复制、前期需要大量时间进行创作，从而对资本吸引力较弱。其次是中国的演艺业现在还处在产业化的初始阶段，资产多以版权和品牌等无形资产居多，传统银行业务难以办理。再次是演艺演出企业对金融知识了解匮乏，金融机构也缺乏对于演艺产业的认知，进而导致演艺和金融之间的信息不对称问题。

四　促进中国演艺对外贸易的建议

中国演艺对外贸易的长期逆差，一方面体现了中国演艺市场旺盛的文化需求，另一方面也反映出自身演艺产品与服务质量参差不齐的现状，既无法满足国内演艺市场不断增长的需求，更不能在国际演艺市场形成有影响力的演艺品牌，占据市场份额。供给与需求的平衡是演艺市场健康发展的前提，长期刺激消费扩大和拉动需求侧的导向使得积贫积弱的演艺市场供给与需求之间的差距越发明显，无法得到满足的演艺需求就转移到了国际演艺产品与服务的供给，从而加剧了中国演艺对外贸易的逆差。面对中国经济发展深入新常态，经济结构不断优化升级，增长动力正从要素驱动、投资驱动转向创新驱动。中国演艺产业也必须着力完善文化产品与服务的

---

① 数据来源：《2015 年文化金融合作取得突破》，《中国文化报》2016 年 2 月 5 日，http://www.mcprc.gov.cn/whzx/whyw/201602/t20160205_460588.html。

供给，实现供给结构的升级，才能突破演艺对外贸易的瓶颈，创造新的发展机遇。

（一）打造中国特色世界驰名院团

建设中国特色世界驰名院团应遵循重视中华民族文化的传承和民族特色、尊重艺术和演艺发展的规律、坚持适应市场规律、坚持对接国际灵活运用文化例外规则、服务于满足人民文化精神需求的原则。

1. 政府政策与市场有效对接

文化发展政策的制定要以有效对接市场为前提，保证政策支持目标单一、清晰，服务于建设统一、开放的文化市场。演艺文化发展政策应关注市场诉求，采用多样化、有针对性和多渠道的支持政策。

2. 构建中国特色国家荣誉制度

建立完善的法律法规，从制度上保障国家荣誉制度的健康运行。坚持开放性和国际化的原则，在国庆节或其他重要传统节日举办庄严、隆重的授予仪式，由国家元首亲自授予勋章、奖章，以示重视和鼓励。

3. 着力打造多元市场主体

不同发展阶段和特色的院团应从市场、企业管理、艺术评价机制等方面有针对地进行调整，实现差异化发展，避免用单一标准评判院团演出与经营成效，以多元化演艺市场供给满足多元的演艺消费需求。营造各类演艺企业一视同仁、公平竞争的发展环境，推动形成不同所有制演艺企业共同发展、大中小微演艺企业相互促进的演艺产业格局。培育一批核心竞争力强的骨干院团，鼓励各类演艺企业以资本为纽带进行联合重组，推动跨地区跨行业跨所有制并购重组，提高演艺产业规模化、集约化、专业化水平。

4. 丰富演艺产品和服务的贸易模式

扩大演艺对外贸易的规模和增强演艺的国际影响力，应丰富和完善演艺产品和服务的贸易模式，实现驻场演出、巡回演出、版权交易、与其他产业的交融互动等多种模式共同发展。

（二）寻求院团体制机制创新

认定部分演艺机构为非营利性组织，发挥政府在非营利性组织资金来源、税收优惠等方面的支持和引导作用，以确保这些非营利组织实现其社会价值。演艺公共文化资源的利用应着力于实现市场主体间资源的均等化与共享，平等对待国有演艺企业和民营演艺企业，让二者都能在演艺文化市场环境中作为独立经济个体健康自由地发展。为避免重复建设、演艺文化资源浪费，建立高效统一的演艺文化设备资源统合平台，促进区域演艺文化设备和空间等资源共享。完善国有院团的退出机制，明确院团生存与发展的不同层次，削减仅能勉强维持生存的院团，整合有发展前景的院团，鼓励、支持自主盈利院团的发展，盘活演艺市场。

对于不具备自我"造血"能力的院团，应建立一套系统的市场退出机制，其中包括：完善评估体系，综合评估院团营运能力、文化影响力、发展难度，以建立院团退出市场的审核标准；健全院团处置措施，对于需要退出演艺市场的院团，采取恢复事业单位、并入其他院团、直接解散等措施，退出市场后人员妥善安置等，为院团退出市场提供健康的退出渠道。市场退出机制的建立在一定程度上可以减少演艺资源和支持资金的浪费，为优势院团创造更大的发展空间。

政策引导社会力量参与公共文化服务建设。一方面，鼓励国家投资、资助或拥有版权的文化产品无偿用于公共文化服务；另一方面，采取政府采购、项目补贴、定向资助、贷款贴息、税收减免等政策，鼓励各类文化企业和经营性文化事业单位参与公共文化服务建设。

（三）构建科学的演艺院团统计与评估体系

逐步取消演艺审批制度，建立事后监管体系，将合理的统计指标体系和评估体系与政府资助和政策扶持相结合，倒逼院团不断提高演出水平。

首先应及时建立中国演艺数据统计平台，摸清全国演艺资源、演艺企业、演艺市场的"家底"。可以借鉴百老汇联盟的周票房制，在各地演艺市场建立数据统计收集和监测试点平台，统筹各级文化主管部门和统计局，逐渐完善对外演出剧目的类型、主创团队、演出票房及演出影响力等要素的备案和数据统计。

科学构建监管和绩效考评体系，真正引导演艺企业进入市场，参与国际国内演艺市场竞争。科学合理设计指标体系，将监管与评价指标切实落在创作、生产、营销等诸多环节上，避免依据场次、数量等指标简单评判国有表演艺术院团绩效，从而推进全面完善的国有表演艺术院团市场化管理体制的形成。依据评估体系，委托专业的第三方社会组织进行公开、公平、公正的评估。待成熟的指标体系建立后，授权演出行业协会等专门的行业组织、机构进行统计数据的收集和院团绩效的评估，并将艺术基金、财政资助、入围重点出口文化企业目录等资金、政策优惠交由行业组织或机构根据评估情况决定适用对象和用途，并统一分配和管理。综合市场要素，将演艺院团的演出绩效和奖励政策挂钩，由第三方进行评估的统计评估体系，不但保证了统计数据的连续性和真实性，更激发了院团专注演出质量和市场效益的动力。

同时进一步完善改进目标考核方法，通过组织专家、消费者参与检查考核、开展社会调查、公布评估结果、新闻媒体监督等方式，提高考核评估的科学性、客观性和监督的有效性。

（四）加强与"一带一路"沿线国家演艺贸易往来

"一带一路"沿线国家与中国地缘位置相近，文化历史相系，理应是中国开展对外演艺贸易的首要合作伙伴，而"一带一路"倡议的提出，不仅搭建了经济、贸易之路，也搭建了文化、友谊的桥梁。由于"一带一路"沿线国家经济发展水平的差异，中国与各国演艺贸易往来必将依据各国演艺市场的成熟度而分区域有序开展。近10年来，中东欧国家文化服务进口需求增长较快，2012年文化服务进口总额达67亿美元，而中国的文化服务进口在中东欧国家不足1亿美元。中东欧地区政治经济相对稳定，文化市场成熟度与中国相当，又地处连接欧亚的枢纽位置，加之中国与中东欧国家形成的"16+1"合作机制，中东欧将成为中国对外演艺贸易的先发腹地。未来中国在对外演艺贸易地理方向上应在持续进驻欧美等成熟文化市场并维持市场份额的基础上，深耕细作东南亚、印度等新兴文化市场，积极探索有潜力的文化市场特别是中东欧国家文化市场。

（五）演艺院团"走出去"借力文化交流

文化贸易是最广义的文化交流。近年来文化交流一直被诟病扰乱了文化市场规律作用的正常发挥，文化交流与文化贸易同为促进中国文化海外传播、提升中国文化影响力的重要手段。一方面，一味依赖文化交流而忽视市场作用不具有可持续性；另一方面，部分资本短缺、盈利空间小的演艺院团单靠自主的市场化运作难以负担海外推广成本，无法将优秀剧目投入国际演艺市场，因而演艺院团应当充分利用文化交流所带来的海外渠道和推广平台，充分认识和了解国际演艺市场，为国际商演铺平了道路。截至 2016 年底中国已在海外建立了30 个中国文化中心，未来这个数字还将不断扩大。海外文化中心所拥有的空间和当地最新市场信息的有效利用可以大大节省院团进行海外推广时宣传场地、渠道获取、市场调研的成本开销。海外中心可以形成固定的机制和品牌来进行优秀演艺产品与服务的展示推介，这样既丰富了海外文化中心的功能，也开拓了演艺剧目的推介渠道。

文化交流与文化贸易相辅相成，政府主导绝对不能代替企业主体，文化交流一定要为文化贸易开道，决不能扰乱市场、干扰市场，甚至破坏市场。演艺院团应该在常年参与文化交流活动的经验当中，培养出以文化交流促进文化贸易的思维，开始利用海外文化交流机会调研海外演艺市场，展示推介优秀的演出剧目或寻找合适的海外合作伙伴。

（六）优化演艺产业的投融资体系

中国的演艺产业现在仍然属于产业化发展的初级阶段，主要以中小企业为主。所以依据实际，中国演艺产业的投融资体系应该进行更合理的顶层设计。

首先，要处理好演艺事业与演艺产业的关系，促进二者协同发展，鼓励演艺事业部门在力所能及的范围内与演艺产业部门在演艺人才的培养、演艺创作的分享、演艺场馆、演艺宣传的合作方面进行直接的协同创新，促使演艺事业和演艺产业共同发展。并且政府对于演艺产业的支持应该更多地体现在融资环境优化上，而非直接的资金支持。因为政府的财政资金有限，所以应该以财政资金为杠杆，撬动更多社会资金支持。通过政府平台的搭建，带动更多的社会资源投入，以及借助非政府组织的力量，提高对演艺产业的管理效率，比如说行业协会，其对于行业内的产业特点、发展态势、竞争状况等具体问题有着更多的经验和了解。加快建设、完善演艺产业投融资体系，推动有关部门落实鼓励和引导社会资本进入演艺产业的各项政策措施，为演艺产业发展持续提供动力。进一步拓宽社会投资的领域和范围，鼓励社会资本进入演艺相关的企业孵化器、众创空间、文化资源保护开发等新兴领域。深化文化金融合作，发挥财政政策、金融政策、产业政策的协同效应，为社会资本进入演艺产业提供金融支持。落实以奖代补、基金注入等重要政策，以推广演艺领域的政府与社会资本合作模式为抓手，扶持引导社会投资进入演艺领域。用好国家投资政策，将演艺领域纳入投资政策工具支持范围。

其次，还应该加速金融创新，来完善投融资品种，构建强大的演艺企业联盟，从纵向和横向两个角度来解决演艺业投融资过程中的信息不对称问题。借助互联网金融平台为演艺产业融资创新提供契机。"众筹"，是一种将团购和预购的模式运用到投融资领域的现象。很多小企业、艺术家或个人借助众筹平台，向公众展示他们的创意理念，同时募集项目启动所需的资金。众筹为更多小本经营企业或热衷于创作的个人提供了实现目标的可能。

（七）完善演艺创作与国际经营管理人才培养机制

中国多年以来的教育体制僵化以及文化管理部门传统地把演艺人才狭义地界定为表演人才，学科与学科之间存在壁垒，艺术院校与普通高校之间在人才培养上几乎没有沟通、合作，亦鲜有共同探讨或研究过交叉学科人才培养问题，导致今天在寻求国际化和市场化发展进程中，极度缺乏演艺创作人才和演艺经营管理人才，而大量的表演人才因演艺品种的属性要求面临转岗、下岗、提前退休等尴尬境地。因此亟待构建完善的演艺人才培养体系，鼓励协同创新和共同发展，培养演艺市场急需的合格人才，以促进演艺企业和演艺市场的良性发展。要继续加强创作人才特别是外向型、复合型高级经营管理人才的培养，以高校为主阵地，以市场为导向，建立高校文化贸易专业人才联动机制。应积极鼓励、扶持高校开设文化贸易专业，聚焦专业课程，形成特色化的课程体系，牢牢把握经济学核心，形成独具特色的专业风格；充分利用高校资源优势，奠定厚实的专业发展基础；坚持产学研一体化的办学模式，打造开放的专业课程体系；同时通过科研项目提高人才培养质量，并利用政、产、学、研各方资源为推动文化贸易人才的合作培养模式建立平台，加大实践课程的培养力度，充分发挥教学实践基地的作用，以包括企业实习等在内的综合形式实现校园教育和演艺行业实践的无缝对接；以应用型为目标，以国际化的视野努力推进专业人才的培养，力求打造熟习国内外演艺市场和对外演艺贸易的全方位人才。

2016 年，国家级、专门性的服务平台从建立走向成熟，加之国家艺术基金的大力支持，为中国演艺市场的发展提供了政策环境和资金支持等各方面的发展新机遇，同时也有诸如统计评估体系等长期忽视的问题变得越发显著，总体上中国演艺市场进入了平稳发展期，这种稳中有增的市场环境是演艺对外贸易顺利发展的必要条件。平稳发展的中国演艺市场，在经过合理优化市场结构和配套政策后必将迎来新的增长点。

第三部分 附录

附录一
国家文化发展国际战略学术服务综合体

一 概述

国家文化发展国际战略研究院是由北京第二外国语学院与原国家文化部文化体制改革工作领导小组办公室于 2010 年共同建立，是致力于国际文化贸易理论与实践研究的专门学术研究机构，研究领域涵盖公共文化事业、文化产业、文化交流与文化贸易、文化遗产传承与发展等。以研究院为核心，相继组建国家文化贸易学术研究平台、首都对外文化贸易研究基地、首都对外文化贸易与文化交流协同创新中心以及京剧传承与发展（国际）研究中心，逐渐形成国际化、综合性的学术研究与服务综合体，研究院承担上述机构秘书处工作（见图 3-1）。

紧密结合国家文化发展的国际战略，北京第二外国语学院自 2003 年起即开启了对文化贸易理论与实践的研究，充分发挥"学术外交"

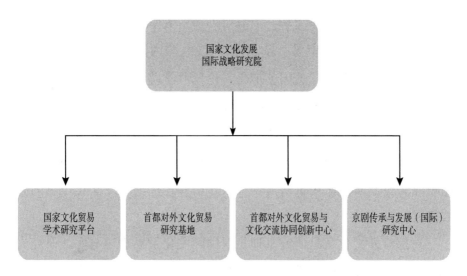

图 3-1　国家文化发展国际战略学术服务综合体示意

独特作用，逐步成为中国文化事业和文化产业国际合作的理论探索者和构建者、实践的学术先行者、政府决策咨询的建议者和推动者、人才培养模式创新的领航者、文化遗产传承与发展的护航者、产业贸易促进的倡导者和服务者。

学术服务综合体承担各级政府部门委托项目，多项学术成果被采纳，直接推动文化贸易相关政策与措施出台；依托国家级重大课题，为深化文化体制改革提供学术支持；梳理各国文化政策法规，推动中国文化管理规制建设。学术服务综合体被誉为"具有工匠精神的学术机构"。特别是首都对外文化贸易研究基地，聚焦首都文化发展的国际战略，2016 年底入选中国智库检索（CTTI）首批来源智库，是唯一以文化贸易研究为特色的入选智库。

国家文化贸易学术研究平台是 2014 年受国家文化部对外文化联络局委托，由北京第二外国语学院牵头，协同中国传媒大学、对外经济贸易大学、中央财经大学、上海对外经贸大学、商务部国际贸易合作研究院以及《国际贸易》杂志社等33家国内高校与研究机构，以及英国纽卡斯尔大学、美国芝加哥哥伦比亚学院、韩国文化产业振兴院、匈牙利贸易署、塞尔维亚国家文化发展战略研究中心等17家海外合作单位共同组建。通过建立国家文化贸易学术研究平台汇聚国内外文化领域资源，创新文化贸易理论实践研究，促进文化产品与服务的跨境交易，加快文化贸易复合型人才培养，推动海外文化市场的有效拓展。

首都对外文化贸易研究基地是以国际文化贸易理论与实践研究为特色的北京市哲学社会科学应用对策研究基地，主要研究内容包括国际文化贸易基础理论、首都对外文化贸易战略政策措施体系、北京文化的国际市场培育与对外贸易拓展、首都文化企业跨国经营与国际化发展四大维度。

首都对外文化贸易与文化交流协同创新中心由北京第二外国语学院作为牵头单位，在国家文化部、商务部等政府相关部门指导下，协同中国国际贸易促进委员会北京分会、北京京剧院、中国传媒大学等文化企业及有关高校、社会组织共同组建。协同中心以服务首都文化发展国际战略的总体目标为导向，以人才培养为核心，以学科建设为基础，以科学研究为支撑，构建人才、学科、科研相互融合的"三位一体"发展模式，以国家文化发展国际战略重大任务和目标为导向。

京剧传承与发展（国际）研究中心由国家文化发展国际战略研究院与北京京剧院共同组建，著名京剧表演艺术家梅葆玖先生生前担任该中心名誉主任。在梅先生的亲自指导和支持下，中心致力于传统艺术的当代表达，通过京剧的品牌化、市场化、国际化，培育国际、国内两个市场，从而推动北京京剧的传承发展与海外传播。

二　主要工作内容与成果

（一）文化"走出去"理论的探索者与构建者

紧密结合国家文化发展的国际战略，自 2003 年起即开启了对文化贸易理论与实践的研究，组建多支务实有效的项目研究团队，以"致用"带动"政产学研"紧密结合，在文化领域多个维度开展理论与实践研究。

（二）文化"走出去"实践的学术先行者

文化产品与服务作为文化"走出去"的现实载体易于被海外受众接纳，对于学术思想与学术观点的认同是对文化更高层次的接纳，承载着更鲜明的文化价值因子，具有更为深远的影响力，也是学术外交的价值所在。在自觉、自主、自愿承担"学术外交"角色的过程中，与海外各方互学互鉴，始终坚持"平等对话，自信表达"，以学术关切为立足点，精准对接产业贸易需求。畅通对话渠道、构建交流机制、平等学术话语权，探路学术力量助力文化"走出去"。

（三）政府决策咨询的建议者和推动者

研究机构以全球文化发展战略的信息智库为定位，展开广视角、多层次的针对性研究，为中国文化发展的国际战略提供信息资源与智力支持。近十几年来研究机构积累了丰富而有价值的研究成果，为政府部门建言献策，多项学术成果直接推动文化贸易相关政策与措施出台，并对出台有关政策的合理性与适用性展开研究，研究成果直接推动了包括 2014 年 3 月国务院《关于加快发展对外文化贸易的意见》

的出台，对加快发展对外文化贸易、推动文化产品和服务出口做出全面部署，明确了推动对外文化贸易工作的指导思想。研究机构还承担多项商务部、文化部、国家文物局等政府部门委托的项目，也通过国家社科基金、北京市哲学社会科学规划办申请研究项目，研究涵盖文化贸易主体、文化贸易发展模式、国际文化贸易路径、文化"走出去"政策、文化市场等多个文化贸易关键领域和环节。

（四）人才培养模式创新的领航者

北京第二外国语学院于 2003 年起就在国内同类专业院校中率先开设了《国际文化贸易热点问题研究》课程，有关国际文化贸易理论与实践研究随即开始。世界范围内文化产业与文化贸易的迅猛发展急需大量国际化、复合型高级经营管理的专门人才，顺应社会经济发展形势，北京第二外国语学院于 2007 年开始招收国际经济与贸易专业（国际文化贸易方向）本科生；2009 年经教育部批准，增设国际文化贸易专业并开始正式招生；2012 年，获批国内首个交叉学科国际文化贸易硕士学位授予权；2016 年，启动国际文化贸易博士后联合培养。至此，北京第二外国语学院已形成了多层次、立体化的国际文化贸易人才培养体系。

1. 推动交叉学科国际文化贸易硕士专业建设

交叉学科国际文化贸易硕士专业已实现多语种、跨学科招生，学生来自中外经济学、管理学、外国语言文学等多个专业背景。国际文化贸易专业旨在培养熟悉国际文化贸易基本理论和实务，通晓国际文化贸易规则、惯例、政策及相关法规，具备国际视野和外语应用能力，具有较高的学术科研水平及创新研究能力，掌握参与文化贸易实践、跨文化沟通技能的国际化、复合型文化贸易人才。借助国家文化贸易学术研究平台的资源优势，组建高校与企业导师组，联动培养急需人才。

2.引领国际联合人才培养模式

与英国、美国、澳大利亚等国高校合作国际文化贸易人才的本科联合培养、本硕连读等模式极大地丰富了文化贸易人才培养的类别并惠及各合作院校与机构，使培养模式不断突破创新。中外合作的本科"1+3"联合培养项目、本硕连读"3+2"等项目突破传统培养模式，构建起适应复合型人才培养的国际化平台。

3.创新政产学研联动的培养机制

构建"政产学研用"一体化教研团队，聘任文化贸易业界专家为产业导师，与学术导师、语言导师共同组建导师组。与完美世界（北京）网络技术有限公司、北京歌华文化发展集团、狮凰文化（北京）有限公司、华谊兄弟、世纪波文化发展有限公司等数十家对外文化贸易优秀企业、机构签署战略合作协议，互设培养基地，创设"完美世界奖学金"等文化贸易专业奖学金，为文化贸易人才培养提供长效机制。

4.培育文化贸易人才成长新常态

推动专业学习与科研实践有效结合，依托研究课题、前沿实践成立学生自我组织与管理的"雏鹰计划"综合平台，吸纳优秀学生组建研究小组，在专家指导下参与科研课题研究与学术活动服务，为优秀学生参与文化贸易研究与实践提供机制化渠道，在更深层次上助力学生成长。

（五）文化遗产传承与发展的护航者

研究团队始终坚持文化贸易与文化交流并重的观点，致力于促进文化产业与文化事业协调发展，通过各类项目从文化贸易研究角度服务文化事业发展，利用市场手段实现文化的国际化以及文化的保护与传承。围绕唱响"北京京剧"品牌、打造北京京剧院成为世界驰名院团这一核心目标，有效推动"北京京剧"的传承、发展及其国际化，为中国传统文化瑰宝"走出去"奠定基础。

1. 共同组建"京剧传承与发展（国际）研究中心"

2012 年 3 月 26 日，国家文化发展国际战略研究院与北京京剧院共同组建"京剧传承与发展（国际）研究中心"。梅派艺术掌门人、著名京剧表演艺术家梅葆玖先生和时任国家文化部政策法规司司长韩永进先生担任研究中心名誉主任，北京京剧院院长李恩杰先生和国家文化发展国际战略研究院常务副院长李嘉珊教授担任研究中心主任，直接推动相关研究及成果落地。

2. 正本清源京剧英译，奠基对外贸易品牌

京剧英文翻译长期使用"Beijing Opera"，在一定程度上将京剧与西方歌剧混淆。经过多位京剧艺术家、语言文字专家、翻译专家、文化专家、经济学家等反复研讨论证，认为将京剧的英文名称音译为"Jingju"是正本清源，可以正确传达出国粹京剧的内涵，准确展现中国文化的特质，在国际传播过程中突出京剧作为一门独特表演艺术的魅力与影响力。在北京京剧院国际商业巡演中，"Jingju"获得外国观众的普遍认可，逐步树立了品牌，为开拓国际演艺市场奠定了基础。

3. 编撰多语种百部经典，扎实传承推广步伐

以北京京剧院百部经典传统剧目介绍为对象编撰的《北京京剧·百部经典剧情简介标准译本》，最难的是保证经典故事简洁讲述，符合国内外观众的阅读需求，同时通过多语种翻译工作的精益求精，促进北京京剧对外传播。在出版过程中，采用 32 开本与口袋书两种形式，以满足不同读者和观众的使用需求。《北京京剧·百部经典剧情简介标准译本》（中英对照）的编撰历时 15 个月，共历经 15 稿，成稿校对 5 次，于 2013 年 9 月正式出版，又陆续出版发布汉德、汉日、汉西、汉葡、汉朝 5 个语种对照版本。

4.搭建文化遗产传承平台，推进京剧国际传播

在"中英创意产业及文化贸易论坛2015"论坛期间，梅葆玖先生随团访问英国，他以"梅兰芳表演艺术对于世界戏剧的贡献"为题发表主旨演讲，在国际学术界影响深远。这是继1935年梅兰芳先生赴英国演出80年后，梅葆玖先生第一次在国际学术讲坛上向世界介绍被国际公认的三大表演体系之一的梅兰芳京剧表演体系对于世界戏剧艺术的贡献。

5.举办机制化高端论坛，助力京剧海内外市场开拓

自京剧传承与发展（国际）研究中心成立起，每年定期举办"京剧传承与发展国际学术论坛"，至今已连续举办五届。论坛汇集政产学研各方，共同为打造"北京京剧"品牌，推动京剧"走出去"建言献策。学术研究成果直接推动北京京剧院"唱响之旅"全球巡演、"传承之旅"全球巡演以及"双甲之约"——重走梅兰芳之路全球巡演等活动。

（六）产业贸易促进的倡导者和服务者

通过体系化、持续性学术研究，为产业贸易实践创新理论、凝练经验。学术机构通过举办机制化活动，如"国际文化贸易论坛""国际服务贸易论坛""文化体制改革与中国文化'走出去'论坛"等年度论坛，搭建产、学、研、用各界专家的互动对话平台，构建起学术服务平台。

1.为文化企业搭建信誉平台

通过主办、参与中外人文交流机制活动，为文化企业连接海外疏通渠道。至今已协同英国、韩国、澳大利亚等国合作伙伴共同主办"创意产业与文化贸易论坛"，在论坛中汇聚国内外文化企业参与相关

话题研讨，分享企业发展的前沿经验、了解最新的政策导向、了解行业发展与跨行业融合的最新动态，表达文化企业自身发展诉求；同时发挥论坛信用保障功能，为国内外文化企业创造相互认知的机会，实现供求有效对接。北京京剧院、华谊兄弟、电影中国、TTF 高级定制珠宝品牌、北京曲剧团、中国演出行业协会、中国国际教育电视台等一批文化机构，通过学术研究平台的国际合作机制联通海外合作伙伴，促成国际合作项目。有效推动了中国与匈牙利动漫电影合作以及中国与罗马尼亚图书版权合作，直接服务文化企业和组织的对外贸易实践。

2. 为文化企业提供人才培训

积极推动文化贸易从业人员培训，为政府部门、文化企业中从事经营管理与对外贸易及文化交流的从业人员服务，并直接参与文化部、商务部组织举办的全国文化贸易培训活动。为北京市、青海省、河南省、南京市等进行文化贸易培训；为北京演艺集团、中国演出行业协会等机构进行文化贸易培训。成功举办"中国－荷兰人文交流项目"，荷兰梵高博物馆与莱茵沃特艺术学院专家为全国博物馆系统人员开展博物馆策展与文物保护人才培训，参与中法博物馆策展人才培训，为中国演出行业协会、中国国际贸易促进委员会北京市分会等社会组织、北京演艺集团等文化企业提供针对性培训。

三　面向未来

国家文化发展战略研究院的战略目标是成为国家文化发展的外脑平台、全球文化发展战略的信息智库、国际文化贸易的理论研究高地、国际文化经营管理人才的培养基地。研究院将继续致力于推进文化产业的国际化与市场化，推动国际文化贸易学术研究的发展。

附录二
中国演出行业协会

一　中国演出行业协会简介

中国演出行业协会^①是中华人民共和国文化部主管的国家一级社会团体，是演出单位和演出从业人员的自律性行业组织。中国演出行业协会成立于1988年，建会之初为中国演出经理家学会，1993年改为中国演出家协会，2012年经民政部批准更名为中国演出行业协会。

中国演出行业协会会员包括演出团体、演出场馆、演出公司、演出经纪公司、演出票务公司、舞台舞美工程企业等单位会员及演出经纪人、演员、编剧、导演等个人会员。全国有28个省级演出行业协会，会员近万名，下设剧场委员会、小剧场戏剧委员会、儿童艺术演出委员会、音乐剧委员会、艺术普及教育委员会、舞美舞台工程企业联盟、演出经纪人联盟、网络表演（直播）分会等分支机构。

中国演出行业协会秉承服务会员、服务行业的宗旨，其主要业务包括：编制《中国演出市场年度报告》，组织编制行业标准；开展行业自律和行业调研活动；提供政策咨询服务、维护会员合法权益，组织演出经纪人等演出从业人员资格认定工作，举办中国国际演出交易会、中国文化产品国际营销年会、国家艺术院团演出推广交易会等，

---

① 中国演出行业协会官网，http://www.capa.com.cn。

建立演出行业信用评价体系，建立演艺产品出口公共服务平台，组织国际文化交流和演出项目推广，推动演出行业的标准化、专业化、规范化、国际化发展进程。

二 中国演出行业协会下设分支机构

（一）中国演出行业协会剧场委员会

中国演出行业协会剧场委员会由全国从事表演艺术的专业剧场、剧院、音乐厅、艺术中心、会堂等演出场所组成，在中国演出行业协会指导下，以社会主义核心价值观为指导方针，遵守宪法、法律及演出法规，制订剧场的行业自律规范，团结成员单位，坚持诚信经营，维护成员合法权益，推动成员之间的协作，解决成员之间的纠纷，促进演出市场的繁荣发展，促进社会主义精神文明建设。

剧场委员会的业务范围包括：开展剧场领域的行业调研，向政府主管部门提供行业建议，推动有利于行业发展的政策性支持；制定剧场行业自律规范，保护会员的合法权益，提供法律咨询服务，维护行业正当利益，促进行业健康发展；开展会员之间的交流活动，组织业务、技术培训，提升剧场经营管理人才水平；促进与艺术表演团体、演出经纪公司等相关行业领域的交流沟通，创新剧场运营模式，推动剧场运营的良性发展；协调不同区域的市场需求和资源配给，推动全国剧场演出的均衡发展；建立与世界主要剧场、艺术节、展会及演艺机构的联系渠道，组织会员参加国际学术交流和业务交流活动。

（二）中国演出行业协会小剧场戏剧专业委员会

中国演出行业协会小剧场戏剧专业委员会由全国范围内从事小剧

场戏剧创作、制作、演出、运营、推广和戏剧教育、培训及小剧场经营管理等与戏剧繁荣发展相关的其他产业团队及个人的中国演出行业协会会员组成，在中国演出行业协会指导下，以习近平总书记文艺座谈会讲话的重要思想为指导方针，以追求真善美的社会主义价值观为核心基础，制订小剧场戏剧领域的行业自律规范，推动小剧场戏剧相关专业领域的标准化建设。

小剧场戏剧专业委员会的业务范围包括：加强会员之间的小剧场戏剧创作交流活动，促进小剧场戏剧创作与区域小剧场之间演出的有效沟通，探索创新小剧场演出与运营模式，推动小剧场创作与运营的良性发展；逐步建立小剧场戏剧发展的自律机制，规范小剧场演出与管理的硬件条件与服务标准，推动小剧场戏剧在制作、演出、运营与管理等方面良性健康的发展，保障会员的合法权益；协调不同区域的演出市场要求和资源优势，建立区域小剧场演出发展的交流平台，推动小剧场戏剧在全国各个区域演出市场的繁荣发展；加强与世界各大戏剧节之间的沟通联系，建立"中国文化走出去"的交流与运营机制，通过"走出去，请进来"，搭建国际戏剧交流平台；组织会员之间的业务、技术交流，将在实践中培养人才与重点办班培养专业人才相结合，奠定小剧场戏剧未来发展创作、制作、运营、管理的人才基础；开展小剧场戏剧领域的行业调查，及时了解和发现小剧场戏剧发展中的矛盾问题，向政府主管部门提供行业建议，促进行业健康发展。

（三）中国演出行业协会音乐剧专业委员会

中国演出行业协会音乐剧专业委员会由全国范围内从事音乐剧创作、制作、演出、运营、推广和戏剧教育、培训及音乐剧专门剧场的经营管理等相关机构及个人的中国演出行业协会会员组成，在中国演出行业协会指导下，以习近平总书记文艺座谈会讲话的重要思想为指导方针，践行社会主义核心价值观，遵守宪法、法律及演出法规，制订音乐剧行业的自律规范，团结成员单位，坚持诚信经营，维护成员合法权益，推动成员之间的协作，协调成员之间的纠纷，促进演出市场的繁荣发展，促进社会主义精神文明建设。

音乐剧专业委员会的业务范围包括：加强会员之间的原创音乐剧创作交流活动，促进制作团体与演出经纪公司、演出场所之间的有效沟通，创新音乐剧演出运营模式，推动音乐剧创作与运营的良性发展；协调不同区域的演出市场要求和资源优势，建立区域音乐剧演出发展交流平台，推动音乐剧在全国演出市场的繁荣发展；加强与世界各大音乐剧节、音乐剧展演、音乐剧学术专业交流等活动的沟通联系，搭建音乐剧国际交流平台；组织会员之间的业务、技术交流，将在实践中培养人才与重点培养专业人才相结合，奠定音乐剧未来发展创作、制作、运营、管理的人才基础；开展音乐剧领域的行业调研，及时了解和发现音乐剧发展中的问题，听取音乐剧全产业链中各环节专业人士的意见，向政府主管部门提供行业建议，申请政策性支持，促进行业健康发展；建立音乐剧媒体公信平台，发布行业动态及成果，为投资者提供专业意见，搭建投资平台，为音乐剧行业注入资本。

（四）中国演出行业协会演员经纪人联盟

中国演出行业协会演员经纪人联盟由全国范围内从事演员经纪的公司及个人会员组成，在中国演出行业协会指导下，以习近平总书记文艺座谈会讲话的重要思想为指导方针，以追求真善美的社会主义价值观为核心基础，制订演员经纪人领域的行业自律规范，推动演员经纪人相关领域的标准化建设；遵守宪法、法律及演出法规，团结成员单位，坚持诚信，维护成员合法权益，推动成员之间的协作，解决成员之间的纠纷，促进演出市场的繁荣发展，促进社会主义精神文明建设。

演员经纪人联盟的业务范围包括：加强演员经纪人之间的交流及经纪人和演出行业其他机构的交流；逐步建立演员经纪人行业发展的自律机制，规范演员经纪人管理服务标准，推动演员经纪人在包装策划、运营与管理等方面良性健康的发展，保障会员的合法权益；协调不同区域的演出市场要求和资源优势，建立演员经纪人发展交流平台，推动演员经纪人在全国各个区域演出市场的繁荣发展；组织会员之间的业务、技术、信息交流，将在实践中培养演员经纪人才与重点办班培养专业人才相结合，加强演员经纪人的从业能力；开展演员经纪行业调查，及时了解和发现演员经纪人发展中的矛盾问题，向政府主管部门提供行业建议，促进行业健康发展；组织演员经纪人年会，树立演员经纪人联盟在演出行业的影响力；为会员提供第三方咨询及演出保障。

（五）中国演出行业协会网络表演（直播）分会

中国演出行业协会网络表演（直播）分会是在文化部市场司指导下成立的，隶属于中国演出行业协会的分支机构，由从事网络直播的互联网平台和从事网络主播经纪的公司组成，旨在正确引导网络直播表演行业生态建设，提升网络直播表演水准与节目质量，推动网络直播行业规范化发展。

中国演出行业协会网络表演（直播）分会的业务范围包括：组织网络直播平台、网络主播经纪公司和线下演出机构及其他相关行业间的交融合作，开拓行业发展空间；组织相关人员培训，提高行业从业者整体素质；搭建会员信息交流与资源共享平台，促进行业良性竞争、共同发展；开展行业调查和研究，及时了解发现行业发展存在的问题和矛盾，向政府主管部门提供政策建议；组织行业年会，开展行业评奖，进行对外宣传，树立网络表演（直播）行业在社会中的正面形象。

附录三
国家数字内容贸易服务平台

中国文化产业协会^① 成立于2013年6月29日，是经国务院批准、民政部登记注册的全国性社会团体。协会会员由国内优秀的文化企事业单位组成，遍及演艺娱乐、论坛活动、网络文化、动漫游戏、影视传媒、工艺美术、文化旅游、文化金融、电子商务等文化领域。自成立以来，中国文化产业协会致力于搭建高层次的国际交流平台，投身教育和公益事业，并且积极开展文化贸易和国际交流，推动中国文化"走出去"。中国文化产业协会还积极参与和组织国际会展活动，引导开展国际并购投资。

"国家数字内容贸易服务平台"是中国文化产业协会牵头组建的公共性服务平台，既包括信息交流、论坛会议、参展参奖等传统平台性业务，更进一步结合"互联网+"，建设运营在线平台，利用数字内容产品所具有的高度标准化、数字化、虚拟化特征，以制作贸易为突破口，打破时间、空间、软件、支付的限制，真正实现在线制作远程管理、在线贸易支付、在线信用等级评价等功能，逐步推动版权贸易、投资贸易，支持国家数字内容企业积极参与国际贸易，打破贸易信息和技术壁垒，响应国家提出的"大众创业"理念，弥补数字内容服务贸易领域的技术及产业空白，实现对外文化贸易的增长。

---

① 中国文化产业协会官网，http://www.chncia.org/xiehuigaikuang.php?mid=10。

一 平台行业地位

磁石云公司于 2016 年建立，因为创新的技术、互联网思维的导入，其被确定为"国家数字内容贸易服务平台"的核心运营单位。国家数字内容贸易服务平台，亦成为"磁石云"平台，是由文化部领导、中国文化产业协会筹建的覆盖全数字内容领域的唯一的国家级平台。"磁石云"平台（简称平台）定位于"第三方、市场化、国际化"，将"互联网+"的模式彻底引入数字内容领域，可彻底改变传统的数字内容贸易生态，迅速搭建起一套完备的服务贸易产业链——建立灵活可定制的个性化生产模式、多人多地任务众包制作模式、远程导演交互模式以及可虚拟化交流的展示模式，在帮助企业快速完成国内外数字化项目内容的同时，实现成本和效率的最优化。

平台采用数字内容服务标准化流程：高端稳定的设备+高效先进的技术+科学合理的行业标准，核心竞争力就是"标准和服务"，平台通过基于云端的远程协作系统建立在线任务分发机制，深入数字内容服务行业，拓展数字服务外包领域，成为维系发包方与服务方的纽带。

二 平台功能

平台通过互联网革新外包制作模式、推出全新的数字监理服务，极大地提升了数字内容制作的效率和便利性。

按照 MPAA 和迪士尼制作的安全规范，创造性地构建了远程云制作系统，最大限度地保障了数字资产和相关知识产权的安全。

平台网站通过大量外包团队的自动筛选和性价比推荐，降低中期和后期制作成本。

公司自建具备世界领先水平的虚拟影棚，提供自主开发的系统性解决方案和实时预览服务。

三　平台领先优势

（一）成熟的"在线云服务"应用平台

目前，世界上数字服务类平台只提供在线注册、信息对接、第三方中介打款等基础服务，没有项目与子项目管理，没有按流程按步骤的项目确认反馈，没有国外同行认同的标准。本平台为 B2B 大型数字服务项目提供完美的解决方案和服务，拥有完整的自主知识产权，可实现用户对项目全流程的远程控制：所有的项目流程都可以在线实施确认，允许项目与子项目的嵌套逻辑，允许项目回滚循环，允许在线远程多人协同制作。这也是目前市场上唯一的工作站级别的数字服务云平台，包括任务发布、协同批注、云支付、数字制片等功能系统。关键环节和流程如下。

1. 制作双方项目接洽

用户通过首页查看推荐项目，对感兴趣的项目，可以继续了解详情，和甲方交流，竞价竞标，直到成功承接项目。

2. 资金结算流程

双方通过任务列表来交流，沟通，提交任务，提出修改意见等。系统会根据任务列表、任务阶段、任务时间等信息，来自动完成资金锁定、任务付款、信息记录的环节，让项目制作双方只关心项目进度，其他的繁复环节都由系统自动处理。

3. 项目制作流程

系统提供独特的确认体系。每一次提交、修改、确认等都由用户确认，并且系统记录备查。仅冻结必要周期资金，项目文件也由系统进行加密处理，这样可以同时维护制作双方的权益。

（二）全新的数字监理体系

平台改革传统制片体系，打造基于互联网的全球数字监理体系。流程中交互确认、支付、数字资产保全、远程桌面操作等将工程监理的理念引入数字制作。平台在其中扮演全程监理、记录、权益保障的角色，确保数据安全，覆盖所有关键的制作流程。

数据资产 100% 安全。允许远程查看数据资产，这就在保护数据安全的同时允许甲乙方 100% 地查看全部数据细节。

覆盖 95% 项目制作流程。除盖章签字部分，所有制作流程（95%）控制都可线上完成。

资料确认效率提高 60%。对制作过程中的步骤确认效率提高60%，而且待确认资料都在云端，便于查找。

全新的数字制片领域。方便制片方通过互联网随时跟进制片进度甚至制作过程，工作效率提升 80%。

（三）以安全为核心的资金保障、数据资产管理机制

平台拥有安全的保护技术标准，重视知识产权保护，提高核心竞争力，现运行中的第三方交易系统和数据资产管理系统符合 MPAA 和迪士尼国际安全规范全面实现：交易安全、协作安全、虚拟化安全、移动性安全。

（四）以创意保值增值为核心 IP 孵化机制

前期展示是吸引投资方的关键环节，当前，中国存有大量的优质剧本，苦于没有制作出极具吸引力的样片、团队资金匮乏等问题。公司计划针对遴选出的 IP 创意，利用低成本、国际化团队、先进的设备和优秀的制作模式等国际化行业产业资源背景，助推文化创意产业成长，并可承担其 Demo 的制作环节，实现其创意的保值增值。

四　平台主要业绩

2016 年，平台完成交易额 1188 万元，完成好莱坞、迪士尼等大型交易项目 6 个，注册企业 108 家，培训人员 700 人，全年应用人次 7300 人次，自主研发平台应用系统及相关技术 15 项，获得软件著作权 7 项，申请专利 8 项，注册商标 1 项，代表天津先后参加了第十二届中国国际动漫节和第十一届中国北京国际文化创意产业博览会。

（一）4K 数字胶片修复项目

平台现已掌握 4K 数字胶片修复的全流程技术方案，已经积累有百余部好莱坞老电影的数字胶片修复项目，拥有国内唯一符合国际标准的修复团队，是美国 MTI 电影公司和中国电影资料馆的长期深度合作伙伴。代表项目 Heidi、Transatlantic、The Front Page、The Mating Call、《盗马贼》、《黄土地》等，主要服务美国 MTI 电影公司、中国电影资料馆、三维六度（北京）科技股份有限公司等多家企业。

（二）动画类项目

动画类项目以渲染和动画调整为主。完成交易额440万，代表项目"一千零一夜"等，主要服务北京河山文化传媒有限责任公司、河山影业（天津）有限公司等多家企业。

（三）影视特效类项目

平台提供DIT、VFX、调色、转码等所有数字后期流程服务，完成交易额410万，代表项目"乌龙未婚妻""超少年密码"等，主要服务华特迪士尼影业中国有限公司、视平方特效有限公司（台湾）等多家企业。

（四）数字制片项目

平台创新打造基于互联网的数字制片体系，合作用户及相关伙伴表示积极关注与支持，试运营期间完成交易额328万。

后　记

　　国家社科基金艺术学重大项目"国有表演艺术院团体制改革现状调查与发展路径研究"（批准号：13ZD05，以下简称重大项目）由北京第二外国语学院副校长李小牧教授担任首席专家，经全国艺术科学规划领导小组办公室审核通过，于2018年3月结项。这是在各方的大力支持下，在国家文化发展国际战略研究院的全力组织和推动下，在项目团队成员的共同努力下取得的重要科研成绩，其顺利结项将产生广泛的学术影响。

　　"国有表演艺术院团体制改革现状调查与发展路径研究"立足于中国作为发展中大国的实际，在全面深化文化体制改革的背景下，对我国国有表演艺术院团体制改革现状进行深入全面的调查研究，并探讨科学可行的发展路径。就学术价值来看，本项目的实施不仅全面深化了对表演艺术院团管理体制、发展机制、国际化战略、市场体系培育与完善相关规律的认识，深化了对表演艺术院团体制改革中所涉及经济规律、管理规律、文化发展规制的认识，而且极大地促进了文化体制改革与创新发展的理论研究以及交叉学科理论的发展和应用。成果特色还体现在应用对策与服务改革导向突出，围绕现实问题解决国有文艺院团改革过程中面临的复杂问题，对国有表演艺术院团体制改革进行多维全面地调研，研究成果极具咨政价值，为政府、企业等相关部门决策提供有力的参考依据。同时该成果学术挖掘与理论分析系统深入，研究了基于文化产品与文化服务本身特殊规律基础之上的演艺院团改革发展的诸多理论问题，对演艺院团改革发展的实践进行了以学术、学理性挖掘和分析为基础的系统探讨，使演艺院团的改革发展研究达到了新高度。

重大项目在首席专家李小牧教授的总体统筹下分为五个子项目，北京第二外国语学院李嘉珊教授担任子项目一"国有表演艺术院团体制改革现状及评估体系研究"负责人；中央文化管理干部学院卢娟副研究员担任子项目二"演艺管理体制改革创新研究"负责人；中央文化管理干部学院毕绪龙研究员担任子项目三"国有表演艺术院团发展机制创新研究"负责人；北京第二外国语学院王海文教授担任子项目四"国有表演艺术院团国际化战略研究"负责人；原中国动漫集团有限公司徐世丕研究员担任子项目五"培育和完善中国演艺市场体系研究"负责人。按照项目研究计划和任务分工，首席专家李小牧教授把握全局，严格履行研究职责，发挥专业优势，与团队共同进行深入的学术挖掘及系统的理论分析，建构起以国有表演艺术院团体制改革为研究对象，以评估体系、管理体制、发展机制、市场体系以及国际化战略为主要内容的研究主体框架。研究过程中，课题组格外重视实地调查，多次参与原文化部全国文化体制改革调研工作，近500人次深入基层院团，获得近200家演艺院团改革发展的实际样本，撰写内部研究报告40余份，研究形成"国有表演艺术院团数据采集分析系统"，获得知识产权认证。

依托重大项目研究，团队撰写提交多份成果要报，高质量成果直面现实问题，多项研究成果被原文化部及北京市有关机构采纳，充分发挥了项目研究的咨政功能。成果要报《以演艺合作为切入点服务国家"一带一路"战略》编入原文化部《文化智库要报》；北京市政协提案《关于北京进一步深化国有院团改革的提案》（提案号0830），被相关部门采纳并出具办理报告，此提案荣获"北京市政协2015年度优秀提案"；《德语国家演艺院团经营管理体制研究》《海外演艺需求市场调查与分析》等多项研究成果获原文化部文化体制改革工作领导小组办公室采纳，受到高度评价，特别是《俄罗斯戏剧文化市场与政策分析》《我国演出票价水平的经济学分析》等部分研究成果刊发于原文化部《文化决策参考》。重大项目研究阶段性成果丰硕，发表学术论文《演艺进出口：贸易标的独特属性及发展趋势》等7篇，编著出版《首都文化贸易发展报告（2015）》《中国特色社会主义文化发展道路研究》《文化改革实践观察》《世界驰名院团发展研究：改革与创新》等著作5部，编撰"北京京剧·百部经典剧情简介标准译本"系列丛书汉英、汉德、汉日、汉韩、汉西、汉葡对照6种语言版本，共12部。阶段性成果数量足、质量高，在决策咨询、调查研究、理论探讨、数据分析以及队伍建设等方面取得了良好的效果。

重大项目研究以北京第二外国语学院交叉学科国际文化贸易研究团队为核心，与中央文化管理干部学院精诚合作，汇聚经济学、管理学、艺术学、哲学、中国语言文学、外国语言文学等近20位多学科专业研究骨干，国内近30位政产学研各界专家，凝练科研方向，拓展研究视野，培养一支特色鲜明、结构合理、充满朝气的交叉学科研究团队。在国家文化贸易学术研究平台和首都对外文化贸易研究基地的支持和推动下，四年间，孵化获得国家级研究项目2项，教育部人文社科项目2项，省部级研究项目8项，培养孵化了地厅级研究项目15项，推动近50人次国际学术交流与合作，国际学术影响力持续发挥。

首席专家办公室和重大项目秘书处设立在北京第二外国语学院国家文化发展国际战略研究院，近四年间严格执行国家社科基金艺术学重大项目的各项管理制度与规范，有序组织学术研讨和实地调研，协调推动政产学研联动研究，高效促进研究成果转化，构建起科学清晰的项目沟通协调机制，形成项目整体开展与子项目具体活动相互配合、互相促进的推进模式，为进行高级别研究项目的管理与服务积累了宝贵的经验。

《中国演艺市场发展报告》（汉英对照）是本项目结项成果之一，由研究团队与中国演出行业协会共同编撰完成。

是以为记。

国家社科基金艺术学重大项目

"国有表演艺术院团体制改革现状调查与发展路径研究"

首席专家办公室

秘书处

2018 年 5 月

Preface

Ancient Silk Road was a link for civilizations in Asia, Europe and Africa. Today, when we promote the implementation of the Belt and Road based on people-to-people bond, cultural communication and dialogue between civilizations are also important. Cultural trade is an effective civil link for the Belt and Road, and countries along are necessarily important for the international trade of performing arts. China's overall economy is doing better. The export of cultural products registered 60.1 billion USD in 2013, making China the largest exporter of cultural products. The "going out" of China's performing arts has transited from cultural exchanges to trade. The foreign trade of cultural products and services, including performing arts, is the "key" to open the besieged city of culture and to channel people's hearts. New opportunities for upgrading the industry, and for quality, effective products have arrived.

The proportion of trade on cultural service, represented by performing arts, in the gross trade volume will increase with the continuous growth of cultural service economy. China's foreign trade on performing arts will further optimize its structure and the performing arts services will achieve positive development on its commercial operation, overseas consumption, cross-border payment and personnel movement. With the increase of China's investment in and trade with countries along the Belt and Road, and the achievements made by China, those countries have greater curiosity for the Chinese culture and Chinese people's way of life, resulting in explosive growth of the demand on China's performing arts products and services. More China's bodies will engage in the trade of performing arts. Government mechanism including Forum on China-Arab Ministers of Culture and China-ASEAN 10+1 Cultural Ministers' Meeting promotes the comprehension of international cultural cooperation mechanism, and will attract more and more state-owned and privately-run troupes, social organizations, intermediary institution and individuals to join performing arts trade. Currently, Chinese culture centers have been established in 11 countries along the Belt and Road and will be trading platforms between the two sides.

The Belt and Road Initiative creates opportunities for the escalation and development of China's performing arts market. China should connect in deeper sense its own performing arts market with those of the countries along the Belt and Road, in accordance with the features of their cultural industry. It is expected that China's growing demand on performing arts will flow out to those countries, and China's performing arts products and services will surly participate more in international competition. Through the conductive mechanism from demand to supply, China's performing arts industry will also undergo the deep supply-side reform. A more completed market will give birth to quality performing arts products and services. A perfected performing arts market in China can express Chinese culture through tradable products and services, thus to lead more peoples to strength the recognition and deepen their understanding on Chinese culture. As such, Chinese culture can achieve its cross age communication with effectiveness.

In the meantime, cultural investment will create a long-term motivation for China's performing arts industry. China will quicken its pace on foreign investment in culture and will also diversify of such investment, in which establishing overseas branches, conducting transnational mergers and acquisitions and signing MOUs will become vital for enterprises' to invest overseas. China's international investment subjects will also be more pluralistic. Not only cultural enterprises, but also those with multi business will also consider cultural industry as an essential field to edge in. Those large manufacturing, real estates and financial enterprises will participate more, based on its abundant funds, in the investment of overseas cultural industry. China's non-financial outbound direct investment has reached 50billion US dollars in countries along the Belt and Road up to now and China's cumulative investment has transcended 18.5 billion US dollars in the 56 overseas economic and trade cooperative zones constructed in 20 countries along. The current capital of investment along the Belt and Road will promote the Chinese multinational enterprises, which already have conducted transactions or industrial investment, to realize the transferring of finances across industries in greater speed. It will also help them better melt into the local performing arts market, in order to build bridges for Chinese performing industry to go abroad into the international performing arts market.

It is noteworthy that the cultural industry of the passing countries on the Belt and Road started to develop in a relatively late time and they develop at a rather slow speed. So the challenges and opportunities are co-existing for China's performing arts to go global. Only by establishing a community of shared interests that is jointly built, and each side jointly undertakes risks and shares profits, only by getting the help from the market to promote the ordered flowing of productive factor sat utmost and to realize the effective distribution of resources,can the performing arts industry of China and the countries along the Belt and Road cooperate and can the cultural market of China and the countries along the Belt and Road deeply integrate. The Belt and Road strategy is bound to be a great undertaking in the worldwide basis with high level and deep connotation. In this road of peace, prosperity, openness, innovation and civilization, the tradeon cultural products, including performing arts, will surly give full play of its distinct advantages, so as to connect the humanistic bond on the Belt and Road. The geographical distance is not insurmountable. If we take the first courageous step towards each other, we can embark on a path leading to friendship, shared development, peace, harmony and a better future.

Comparing to other cultural products and services, performing arts performances and services possesses the economic features including suffering the least from modern technology, not being much influenced by modern capital and developing in a rather limited space to expand industrial scale. Performing arts and services, meanwhile, bears the core cultural value of certain countries and regions. So people will be unconsciously influenced by it to feel and agree with the content and emotion expressed by it thus they will receive an emotional education and relieve their pressure with enjoyment. Therefore, trades on performing arts are indeed a wise approach to spread Chinese culture abroad. *The report of China's Performing Arts Market* is compiled by specialized team of the National Institute of Cultural Development of international strategy, at the moment that the Belt and Road initiative has brought new opportunities to boost the foreign trade of China's performing arts. It aims to present the development of China's performing arts market during the 12th Five-Year, which are critical five years for the development of China's cultural industry, in both Chinese and English. The report will also summarize and analyze the development of China's performing arts industry and foreign trade on performing arts in 2016. We hope that this report could serve as windows to the outside world to get acknowledged with China's performing arts industry and its foreign trade. We hope that this report could let more governments, enterprises, academic institutes and people in more countries and regions to find out the enormous consuming potential of China's performing arts market, while this report could also continue serving the development of China's foreign trade on performing arts. We also hope that this it could help China's performing arts industry find more international cooperation and draw the blueprint of trade on performing arts with countries on the Belt and Road.

Compiler

2018. Spring

Part I

Overview on China's Development in the Industry of Performing Arts during the 12th Five-Year (2011-2015)

Under the influence of the "Frugality Order", China's performing arts market has been undergoing gradual changes during the 12th Five-Year (from 2001 to 2015). The Chinese performing arts market that used to seem prosperous is squeezing out the bubbles and developing towards a more comprehensive one. Under the new situation that the changing performing market is filled up with increasingly fierce competition, some performing arts troupes have actively seized this opportunity and expand their consumers, which have brought about fair economic profits and social benefits. During the 12th Five-Year, the Chinese government has carried out a series of preferential policies on optimizing the environment of cultural development, in the aim of promoting the cultural prosperity. These include the *Opinions on Accelerating the Development of Foreign Trade in Cultural Products* issued by the State Council, *Opinions on Further Promoting Cultural and Financial Cooperation* issued by the Ministry of Culture, the People's Bank of China, and the Ministry of Finance, *Notice on Relevant Issues Concerning the Preferential Policies of Enterprise Income Tax Applicable to Small Meager-profit Enterprises* authorized by the Ministry of Finance and the State Administration of Taxation, *Implementing Opinions on Vigorously Supporting the Development of Small- and Micro-Sized Cultural Enterprises* authorized by the Ministry of Culture, the Ministry of Industry and Information, and the Ministry of Finance, etc. These policies have solved the practical problems of cultural enterprises during their development and have also brought new opportunities for them to develop.

Steady progress has been made on the reform of the cultural system in which that of the state-owned performing art troupes is still the work of priority. The way of supporting the development of the cultural and art industry has changed to a large extent, from directly allocating money to buying the services by the government, subsidizing the innovative plays and replacing allowance by giving rewards. All those policies are for encouraging the innovation and production of performing art enterprises, improving their capability of serving the public and recognizing the market trend. General Secretary Xi Jinping has indicated the direction of advance for the future literary creation through his speech at the Forum of Art and Literature. He instructs writers and artists to shoulder the historical obligation, to insist on orienting people as sources of creation, so as to contribute the people more works worthy of the times. The Chinese government will further streamline its administration and decentralize its power, and strength the regulations of examination and approval, with the aim of invigorating the market, as well as making administration more regulative, transparent and fair.

From an international perspective, with the development of the world multi-polarization, economic globalization, cultural diversity and society informatization, the status and role of culture in international communication are more prominent. The Belt and Road initiative has brought many cultural cooperation mechanisms and guarantees, and has created infinite possibilities for China's cultural industry and its foreign trade, including performing arts.Meanwhile, the exchange of ideas and cultures worldwide is more frequent, the competition of comprehensive national strength is more intense, the situation of cultural security is more complex, which caused the task of improving the soft power of national culture and enhancing the international discourse power is also increasingly urgent. As an important part of culture, the performing industry is facing great development opportunities and many challenges as well.

China's performing arts industry is under growth and upgrading during the 12th Five-Year. It is developing as a whole towards a more optimized and stable one.

1. A Continuous Growth in Business Scale

1.1 A Marked Increase in Performing Arts Troupes

The 12th Five-Year has witnessed a marked increase in performing arts institutes. There are 7,055 performing arts troupes and 1429 performing arts venues in 2011. While there are 7321 performing arts troupes and 1,279 performing arts venues in 2012, which has achieved an increase of 3.77% and a decrease of 10.50% respectively comparing to 2011. There are 8,180 performing arts troupes and 1,344 performing arts venues in 2013, which increased 11.73% and 5.08% respectively than 2012. While the numbers become 8,769 and 1,338 in 2014, with an increase of 7.20% and an decrease of 0.45% comparing to 2013. While in 2015, the numbers change into 10,787 and 2,143, rising 23.01% and 60.16% respectively (Chart 1-1 and Chart 1-2).

Overall, both troupes and performing arts venues have maintained a fairly stable and continuous growth trend. The total number of performing arts institutes has increased from 8,484 in 2011 to 12,930 in 2015, with an annual growth rate of 11.54%. The year 2015 has witnessed the quickest annual growth of that, which reached 27.93%, as well as that of the number of performing arts venues, which ran up to 27.93% (Chart 1-3). [1]

---

[1] 数据来源: 国家统计局社会科技和文化产业统计司、中宣部文化体制改革和发展办公室,《中国文化及相关产业统计年鉴》, 中国统计出版社。

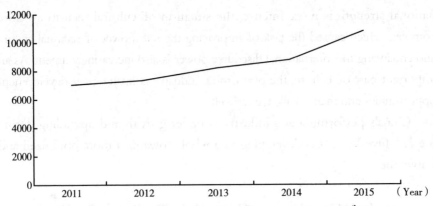

Chart 1–1   The Number of Performing Arts Troupes during the 12ᵗʰ Five–Year

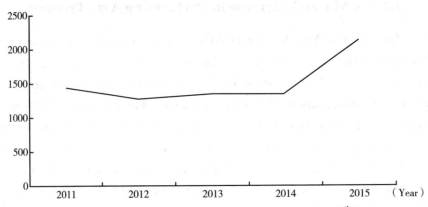

Chart 1–2   The Number of Performing Arts Venues during the 12ᵗʰ Five–Year

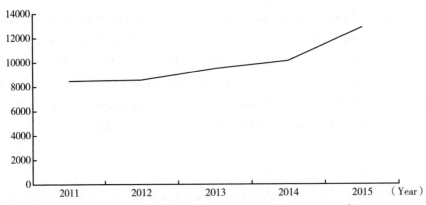

Chart 1–3   The Number of Performing Arts Troupes during the 12ᵗʰ Five–Year

1.2 A Fluctuating Rise of Performances

The number of performances has increased in fluctuation during the 12th Five-Year. Chinese performing arts troupes have in total given 1,550,000 performances and performing arts venues have held 562,000 performances during the 12th Five-Year. Chinese performing arts troupes have given 1,350,000 performances in 2012, which have fallen 12.90% comparing to 2011.The performing arts venues have held 575,000 performances in 2012, which have increased 2.31% comparing to 2011. Chinese performing arts troupes have given 1,650,000 performances in 2016 and performing arts venues have held 829000 performances in 2013, increasing 22.22% and 44.17% than 2012. Chinese performing arts groups have put on 1,740,000performances in China in 2014, which have risen 5.45% than 2013. The performing arts venues have held 781,000 performances in 2014, which have decreased 5.79% than 2013. In 2015, the performing arts groups have given 2,110,000 performances, and the performing arts venues have held 1,065,000 performances, which increased 21.26% and 36.36% respectively comparing to 2014 (Chart 1-4 and Chart 1-5).

The performances from performing arts groups and in performing arts venues have presented fluctuation in different degrees during the 12th Five-Year. Although the total number of performances has declined in a small scale in 2012, it has presented an overall stable increase in the five years. From

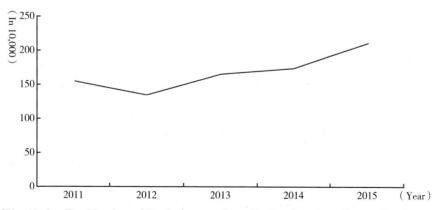

Chart 1–4　The Number of Performances from Performing Arts Groups During the 12th Five–Year

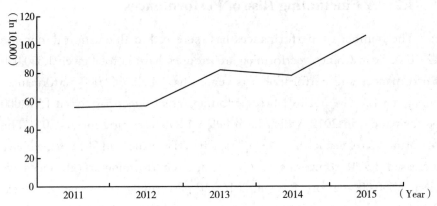

Chart 1-5   The Number of Performances Performed(Played) in Performing Arts Venues During the 12th Five-Year

1,925,000 in 2012 to 3,175,000 in 2015, the total performances have achieved an average annual growth rate of 11.89% in the 12th Five-Year, during which the year 2013 has seen the quickest growth at 28.78% (Chart 1-6).

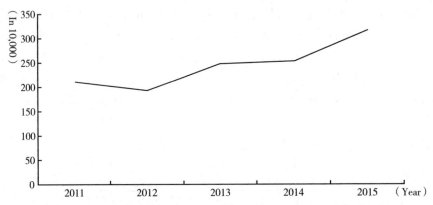

Chart 1-6   The Total Number of Performances During the 12th Five-Year

1.3   A Continuous Growth on Audiences

The 12th Five-Year has also seen a continuous growth of the audiences watching performing arts. There are in total 815,120,000 audiences in 2011, including 745,850,000 audiences for performing arts troupes and 69,270,000audiences coming to performing arts venues. There are in total 889,047,000 audiences in 2012, including 828,050,000audiences for performing arts troupes and 60,997,000 audiences coming to performing arts venues, rising 9.07% than 2011. There are in total 978,403,000 audiences in 2013, including 900,640,000 audiences for performing arts troupes and 77,763,000 audiences coming to performing arts venues, which increased 10.05% than 2012. There are in total 978,644,000 audiences in 2014, including 910,200,000 audiences for performing arts troupes and 68,444,000 audiences coming to performing arts venues, which increased 0.02% than 2013. There are in total 1,065,744,000 audiences in 2015, including 957,990,000 audiences for performing arts troupes and 107,754,000 audiences coming to performing arts venues, which achieved an increase of 8.9% than 2014. From the continuous growth of audiences, we can see that more and more Chinese consumers have begun paying attention to and also watching performing arts. The audiences for performing arts market have been gradually cultivated (Chart 1-7).

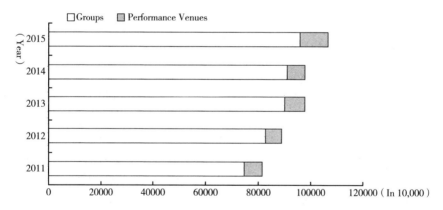

Chart 1–7   The Total Number of Audiences of Performing Arts During the 12ᵗʰ Five–Year

2. An Expansion of Employees Scale

The number of employees working in the performing arts industry has achieved a remarkable leap. From 253,079 employees in 2011, including 226,599 employees in performing arts troupes and 26,480 employees in performing arts venues, to 348,612 employees in 2015, including 301,878 employees in performing arts troupes and 46,734 employees in performing arts venues, employees working in the performing arts industry have expanded their numbers and scale for almost 37.75% in the five years. With the constant developing of China's performing arts market, the expansion of employees is beneficial to the output of performing arts industry (Chart 1-8).

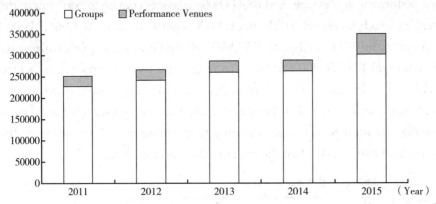

Chart 1–8   The Number of Employees in the Performing Arts Industry During the 12th Five–Year

During the 12th Five-Year, the growth rate of employees working in performing arts troupes and performing arts venues is much higher than that of those in China's whole market and China's third industry. The number of employees working in performing arts troupes and performing arts venues transcends annually in a large degree that of those in China's whole market and China's third industry, except 2014. The number of employees working in performing arts troupes and performing arts venues develop in an average annual growth rate of 8.58%, while the number of employees in China's whole market and China's third industry grow annually only 0.34% and 4.76% respectively (Chart 1-9).

3. A Soar/ Remarkable Growth of Investment in fixed assets

The real used area of constructions by performing arts troupes has increased

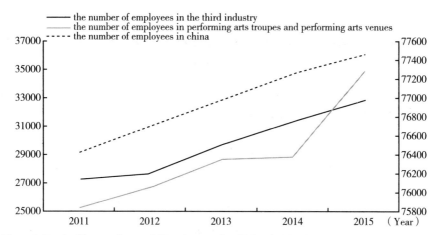

**Chart 1–9   A Comparison of Employees in China's Market, The Third Industry,
Performing Arts Troupes and Performing Arts Venues During the 12th Five–Year**

rapidly during the 12th Five-Year. The real used area of constructions is 5,260,000
square meters in 2011, while that is 6,170,000 square meters in 2012, increasing
17.30%. The real used area of constructions is 6,380,000 square meters in 2013,
increasing 3.4% than 2012. The real used area of constructions is 7,160,000 square
meters in 2014, increasing 12.23% than 2013. The real used area of constructions
rises to 8 million square meters in 2015, increasing 11.73% than 2014. The soaring
of the real used area of constructions for performing arts troupes indirectly
reflects the growth of investment in fixed assets in the performing arts industry
during the 12th Five-Year (Chart 1-10).

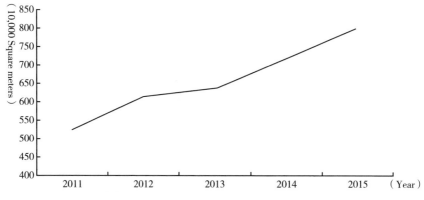

Chart 1–10   The Real Used Area of Constructions by Performing Arts Troupes

4. A Fluctuating Growth of the Profits of Performing Arts Enterprises

4.1 A Slight Fluctuation of the Total Economic Scale of the Performing Arts Market

The economic scale of China's performing arts market has kept an annual growth at 19.82% during the 12th Five-Year, which is a very remarkable speed. The economic scale of the national performing arts market is 23,330,000,000 RMB in 2011 and it increased to 35,590,000,000 RMB in 2012. In 2013, this figure has increased to 463 million, while in 2014, the national economic scale of the performing arts market has endured a slight declination, falling to 43,432,000,000 RMB, but the scale has picked up again to 46,659,000,000 RMB in 2015 (Chart 1-11). [1]

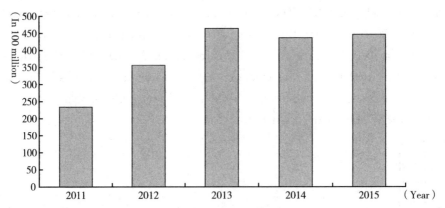

Chart 1–11　The Total Economic Sale of the Performing Arts Market During the 12th Five–Year

---

[1]　Data Sources: China Association of Performing Arts, *Annual Report of China Performance Marker*. The Theater's annual subsidy income and entertainment performance income are both included in the statistical scope of the performance market's overall economic scale since 2013.

4.2   A Structural fluctuation of the Box Offices of Performing Arts Performances

China's box offices of performing arts performances, including performances in professional theaters, large vocal concerts, music festivals, tourism, and as entertainment in performing arts venues, have presented an overall growing trend during the 12th Five-Year. The national box offices for performing arts have reached 10,530 million RMB in 2011, and it has risen 28.2%, reaching 13,500 million RMB in 2012. It has increased 25% in 2013 than 2012, reaching 16,879 million RMB. The national box offices for performing arts have slightly fallen 12.1%, to 14,832 million RMB in 2013, after rapidly growing for two years, while it has risen 9.0% picking up back to 16,172 million RMB in 2015 (Chart 1-12).

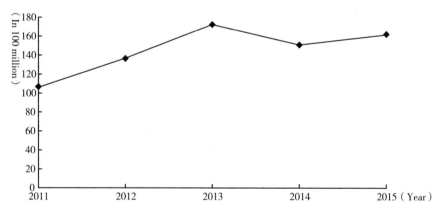

Chart 1–12   The Box Offices of Performing Arts Performances During the 12th Five-Year

The gross box offices of performing arts performances has presented a stable growth trend during the 12th Five-Year. Meanwhile, the box offices for different kinds of performances have, however, appeared a distinct difference. The performance in professional theaters remains the most stable growth rate, as well as the one with the highest box offices. The performance in

109

tourism has appeared the highest fluctuation comparing to other kinds. It has increased and again fallen, both in a large degree, in 2013 and 2014. While, the box offices of performance in large vocal concerts, music festivals, and entertaining performances in performing arts venues have been in a similar level. One wanes while the other waxes (Chart 1-13).

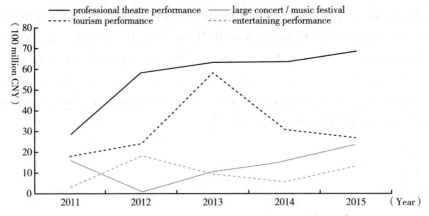

Chart 1-13   Box Offices for Various Performances During the 12th Five-Year

Table 1-1   The Distribution of Box Offices for Various Performances during the 12th Five-Year

(100 million CNY)

Year	Total Income	Performances in Professional Theaters	Performances in Large Vocal Concerts and Music Festivals	Performances in Tourism	Performances as entertainment in performing arts venues
2011	105.30	36.70	25.50	27.80	15.30
2012	135.00	61.20	13.30	32.70	27.80
2013	168.79	65.37	21.36	61.20	20.86
2014	148.32	66.09	25.69	38.37	18.17
2015	161.72	70.68	31.80	35.17	24.07

Data Sources: China Association of Performing Arts, *Annual Report of China Performance Market.*

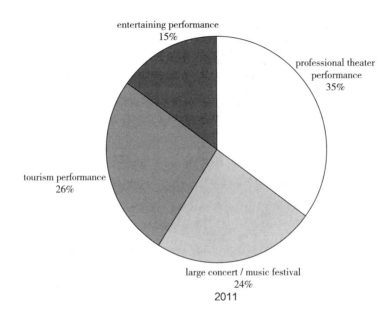

entertaining performance
15%

professional theater
performance
35%

tourism performance
26%

large concert / music festival
24%

2011

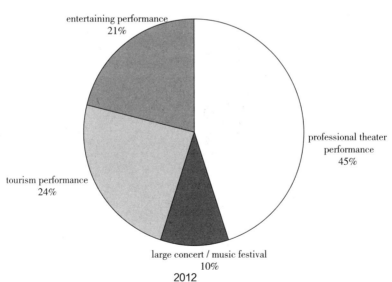

entertaining performance
21%

professional theater
performance
45%

tourism performance
24%

large concert / music festival
10%

2012

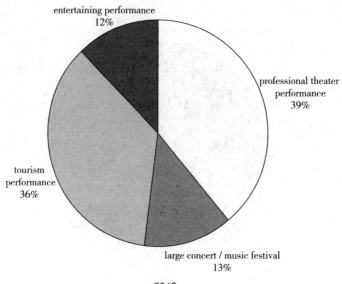

entertaining performance
12%

professional theater
performance
39%

tourism
performance
36%

large concert / music festival
13%

2013

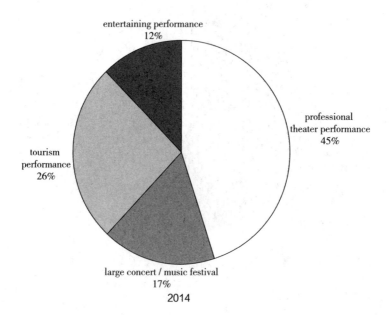

entertaining performance
12%

professional
theater performance
45%

tourism
performance
26%

large concert / music festival
17%

2014

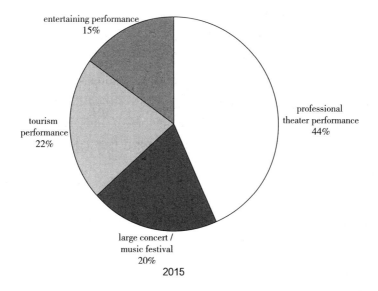

entertaining performance
15%

tourism
performance
22%

professional
theater performance
44%

large concert /
music festival
20%

2015

Chart 1–14   The Change of Box Offices during the 12th Five–Year

Data Sources: China Association of Performing Arts, *Annual Peport of China Performance Market.*

4.3   An Inequality of Incomes between Performing Arts Troupes and Theaters

China's performing arts industry has been creating profits by a large margin during the 12th Five-Year, realizing an annual growth rate at 19.84%. Performing arts troupes have always been creating the highest income, consisting of over 75% of all the income in the industry in all the five years. The total income of the performing arts industry has reached 18,063,620,000 RMB in 2011, including 15,402,630,000 RMB created by performing arts troupes and 2,660,990,000 RMB by performing arts theaters. The figure has raised up to 25,286,830,000 RMB in 2012, including 23,104,600,000 RMB created by performing arts troupes and 2,182,230,000 RMB by performing arts theaters. In 2013, the total income is 32,266,270,000 RMB, including 28,002,660,000 RMB created by performing arts troupes and 4,263,610,000 RMB by performing arts theaters, increasing 27.60% than 2012. In 2014, the total income is 26,677,450,000 RMB, including 22,640,460,000 RMB by performing arts troupes and 4,036,990,000 by performing arts theaters, falling 17.32% than 2013. The total income in 2015 is 34,441,290,000RMB, including 25,764,990,000 RMB created by performing arts troupes and 8,676,300,000 RMB by performing arts theaters, rising 29.10% than 2014. The incomes of the performing arts industry and the number of audiences have shown a basically similar change during the 12th Five-Year (Chart 1-15).

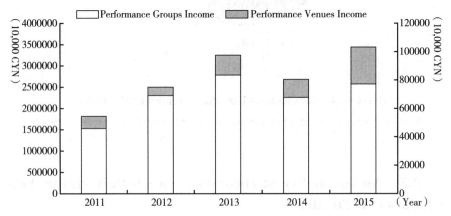

Chart 1–15   The Income of Performing Arts during the 12th Five–Year

Under comparison, the performing arts troupes appeared more activity than performing arts venues, shown from stronger motivation to produce plays. Performing arts venues create profits mainly through renting out theaters to hold performances from performing arts troupes, which leads to the result that the performing arts troupes always earn more than them. But even if performing arts troupes comprised much of the total income of performing arts industry, their profit rate is actually not very high. The average profit rate of performing arts troupes is only 9% during the 12th Five-Year. (Chart 1-16)

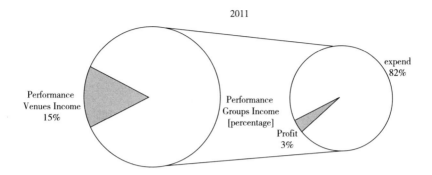

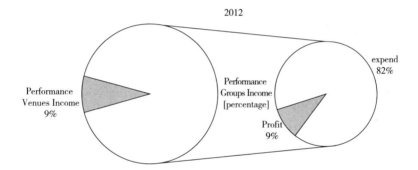

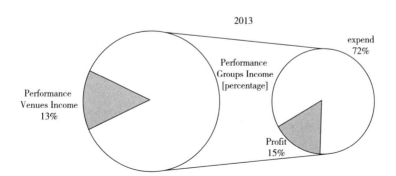

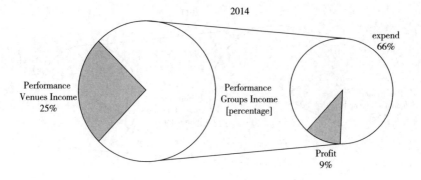

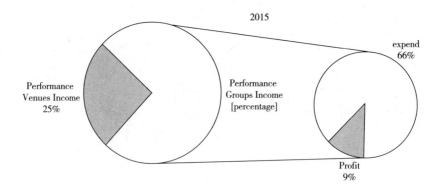

Chart 1–16　The Ratio of Different Performing Arts Incomes

Data Sources: Social Science and Technnology and Cultural Industry Statistics Division of National Bureau of Statistics of the Peaple's Republic of China, Office of Reform and Develop of Cultural Administrative System of Publicity Department of the communist party of China, *Statistical Yearbook of Chinese and Related Industries*, China Statistical Publishing House.

Part II

The Report of the 2016 China's Performing Arts Market

The year 2016, as the starting year of the 13th Five-Year, has witnessed a continuous steady growth of China's performing arts market. Although the market has still been undergoing transformation in its structure, its relative industries has gradually integrated with each other in deeper sense. The performing arts market in metropolitan cities, whose status and influence have gradually shown clear, has radiated its effect out to those in other cities across China. Numerous sums of finance also keep flooding into the performing arts market.

As for foreign trade on performing arts, imported plays are still a motivator for Chinese performing arts troupes to learn from. Meanwhile more and more attention is paid to the marketization of performing arts. Large-scale cultural exchange programs are seeking transition. What's more, China has begun setting up systematic service platform and funding base of performing arts, so as to provide insurance for performing arts troupes to go global.

1. The Features of the Development of China's Performing Arts Market

China's performing arts has presented in total 18,310,000 plays in 2016, which cultivated a market with an economic scale of 46,922 million RMB (Chart 2-1). Although the number of performances fluctuates a bit over the past six years, the overall performing arts market is still developing with an optimistic trend. China's performing arts market has shown with some features, such as integrating across industries, first line cities radiates its influence out across China, etc. under this stable market. Thus, the performing arts markets in different cities are getting related together in deeper sense.

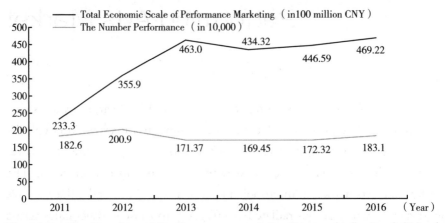

Chart 2–1   The Number of Performances and the Economic Scale of China's Performing Arts Market from 2011 to 2016

1.1   The Constant Growth of the Profits of Performing Arts Market

China's performing arts market has expanded its economic scale to 46,922 million RMB in 2016, increasing 5.7% comparing to 44,659 million RMB in 2015. The economic scale has remained expanding for three years straight. Specifically, the performances in movie theaters have created profit, including the distributed share from tourism (Chart 2-2), of 16,809 million RMB, increasing 3.93% than 2015. The performances in villages have created profit of 2,424 million RMB in 2016, increasing 8.6% than 2015. The entertainment performances have created profit of 7,103 million RMB in 2013, increasing 2% than 2015. The derivative products and sponsorship has created income of 3,157 million RMB in 2016, increasing 7.97 % than 2015. The supporting facilities of businesses and other services have created profit of 5,454 million RMB, decreasing 1.25% than 2015. The government's subsidies, not including the subsidies to villages for the benefit of the people, have contribute to 11, 974 million RMB in 2016, increasing 10.42% than 2015.

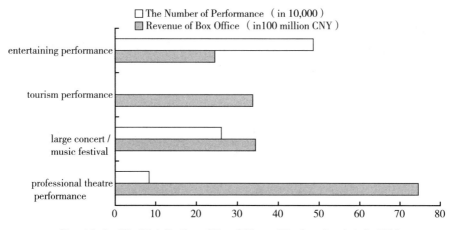

Chart 2–2　The Distribution of Box Offices of Performing Arts in 2014

China's performing arts market has created more income in 2016 than the peak value of 46,300 million RMB in 2013, expanding the market to the largest economic scale in the past six years. The performing arts sites have shown a precious increasing trend in three years straight, which is a rare phenomenon in the past. It is truly valuable for China's performing arts market, which often appears fluctuations in development, to have that many optimistic growth. It also approves that China's performing arts market has indeed kept its stable growth trend in recent years. The stable development of China's economy has provided insurance for performing arts troupes to make innovation; it also enhanced the capability of the performing arts market to resist risks.

1.2 Distinct features of Different Performances

China's performing arts avenues have held 1,831 thousand performances in 2016, increasing 6.26% than 1,723,200 performances in 2015. The total number of performances in China's performing arts market has remained the same in each year from 2011 to now, but the number of performances of a concrete kind of performing has been frequently changing, as shown from Chart 2-3. The income of performances has even been changing up and down with higher frequencies. Those fluctuations in the number of performances and performing income began to be calm down in 2014, remaining a small-scale of fluctuation or turning into positive growth (Chart 2-4).

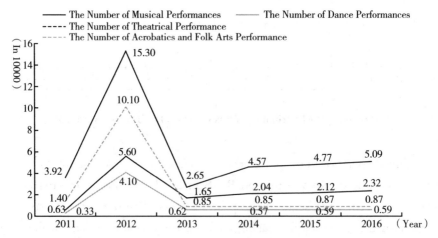

Chart 2–3 Changes of the Number of Performances of Different Plays in China From 2011 to 2016

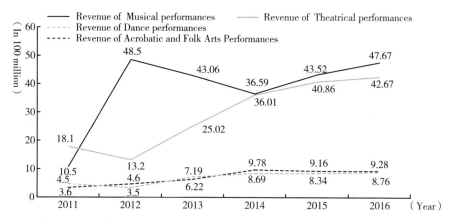

Chart 2–4   Changes of Income of Different Plays in China From 2011 to 2016

1.2.1 Musical Performances

1.2.1.1Concerts

The concert performances have expanded its market in a large degree in 2016. There is a large elevation of its number of performances in professional theaters and box offices. It is shown of its effect of popularizing art among the public and cultivating a concert market.

Table 2–1   A Comparison between the Concerts' Performance Market in 2015 and 2016

Content	2015	2016	percentage (%)
Performances (in 10,000)	1.93	2.11	9.33
Average Price (CNY)	143	150	↑
Attendance Rate (%)	71	85	↑
Number of Audiences (in 10,000)	547.51	627.73	14.65
Box Office (in 100 million CNY)	11.72	12.79	9.13

International symphony orchestra gave quality and frequent performances in China. The year 2016 has witnessed a lot of international symphony orchestra coming to Beijing for performance. Almost every month China welcomes orchestras with international influence, including Vienna Philharmonic Orchestra, Philadelphia Orchestra, Saint-Petersburg Academic

Philharmonic, Dresden Philharmonic, Poland Warsaw Symphony Orchestra, San Francisco Symphony Orchestra, etc. Only in January of 2016, China's National Center of Performing Arts has welcomed Zubin Mehta, Riccardo Mutti, Christoph Eschenbach and Patrick Loyd leading The Israel Philharmonic, Chicago Symphony Orchestra, The schleswig-Holstein Festival Orchestra and Radio Symphonie Orchester Wien respectively for performances.

The fact that international symphony orchestras visit China for performances with such a high frequency proves that, firstly, China's performing arts market has gradually become mature, shown from its economic power and facilities to invite those international symphony orchestras to China; secondly, Chinese audiences for performing arts have expanded with higher appreciation. These two developments both contribute to the willingness of international Symphony Orchestras to perform in China. The number of audiences in concerts has increased 14.56% in 2016 than 2015, with over 85% of attendance rate.

Medium-scale and small cities have gradually cultivated their performing arts market. With the construction of theaters in local cities, and the gradual saturation and intense competition in performing arts markets in metropolitan cities, many concerts have begun to transfer to medium-scale and small cities. For example, Beijing Symphony Orchestra has cooperated with Poly Theater to give performances in 14 medium-scale and small cities, including Changshu, Yixing, Kunshan, Wuhan, and Changsha in the latter half of 2016.Pianist Li Yundi has also chosen some medium-scale and small cities, such as Huizhou, Weihai, Weifang, Zhoushan and Kunshan, as destinations of his performing tour. Conductor Yu Long and musician Ma Youyou and Wu Tong have also cooperated with orchestras in Xi'an, Lanzhou, Urumqi to put on performances together. Those famous orchestras and famous artists are willing to give performances in medium-scale and small cities, which will surely further expand the market of concerts there and cultivate more local audiences.

the concerts have been constantly innovating their content with integration of classic and modern and with collision between tradition and fashion. The content of concerts is never confined to traditional classics, but are becoming diverse. Concerts about movie music, animation and comic music and game music have attracted a new group of audiences. Mash-up performance has also become a new way of innovation. For example, Beijing Chinese Orchestra has performed a multimedia sit-concert *Five Elements*, which combines flute, Xiao (vertical bamboo flute), Xun (oval earthenware wind instrument with six holes) and other Chinese national instruments with human voice, percussion instruments and electronic music to create different audio-visual experiences. Shanghai Concert Hall has also organized the "Endless Music" festival, which has brought new interpretation to music by mashing up classic music and electronic music, music and dance opera music.

Innovation has brought new attention to concerts in the information era. Such innovation include for example, the "Exquisite Traditional Chinese Music" concert, performed by Shanghai Xinyi National Orchestra, allows audience to take pictures on the scene. Other innovations include that the *Doraemon* (robotic cat), and *Smooth Criminal*, the classic song from Michael Jackson, performed by Chinese traditional instrument, have attracted huge attention from netizens after uploaded into the Internet. What's more, the encores *Zhang Shichao, Where Did You Put my Keys?*' and *So Far, the Sofa is So Far*, given by the Rainbow Chamber Singers during its encores have become a hot topic of the moment on the Internet, due to its humor and realism, which has given rise to a lively debate. Those innovations match with the taste of young audiences, which could seek and cultivate more audiences for concerts.

1.2.1.2　Vocal Concerts

The vocal concerts and music festivals have given performances of 2100 times in 2016, rising 10.53% than 2015. They have created box offices of 3,488 million RMB, rising 9.69% than 2015.

The performances from stars have a high cost, which pushes up ticket prices. Statistically, if stars hold vocal concerts in large stadiums, the lowest price in average is 300 RMB in 2016, while the highest price in average is 1300 RMB. But the superstars who could appeal a high box office usually hold vocal concerts with even higher prices. For example, the price range for Jay Chou's a performing tour in Beijing is 580 to 2280 RMB, for

Jacky Cheung's performing tour in Beijing is 580 to 1880, for Eason Chan's performing tour in Beijing is 380 to 1980, while for Faye Wong's Shanghai vocal concert in 2016, which has brought into sharp focus, is 1800 to 7800.

The direct reason for the high prices the high cost of performances, which first includes the expensive appearance fee of stars and their teams, and then includes the basic renting fee of the stadium, fees of stage construction, lighting, stereo set, and security. A vocal concerts needs investment of millions and tens of millions RMB, while the high cost will be ultimately turned into high prices on consumers. What's more, working tickets, complimentary ticket and other up sold tickets will bring invisible cost, which will also pushes up the prices indirectly.

Vocal concerts in theaters with low cost and low risk sprung up in recent years. In recent years, singers who are relatively known with small groups of people have often chosen theaters to hold their vocal concerts, which have gradually become a trend. For example, Cheer Chen, Chenli, Escape Plan, HANGGAI and other singers and bands all chose their 2016 performing tour in professional theaters. Comparing to large stadium, holding vocal concerts in theaters bears the advantages of low investment, controllable cost and relatively low risks. The investment of a performance in theater is from hundreds of thousand to one million RMB. Statistically, the lowest price in average for vocal concerts in theaters is 180 RMB in 2016, while the highest price in average is 800 RMB.

Most singers do not have the enough appealing of box office to give performances in large stadium in a high frequency. So holding a performing tour in theaters is a new way for them to spread their music and increase their fans. But giving performances in theaters also ask singers to change their thought of "only singing in large vocal concerts" and operative agencies to abandon their attitude towards profits as"doing business once in three years for earning profits of three years", but reasonably planning their performances with low profits for big quantity and for enriching the supplies of cultural products.

The Internet went deep into the operation of vocal concerts. With the deep going of the Internet into the operation of vocal concerts, online live shows have become an necessity of vocal concerts. The income from copyright has also become a significant part of profit of vocal concerts. The number of audiences who choose to watch the live shows online has been increasing in a large scale in recently years. Tencent LiveMusic channel has covered live shows of more than 400 performances in 2016, with over 2 billion cumulative playing times and over 600 million covered audiences. For example, the Faye's Moments Live 2016, which was also given live show in Tencent LiveMusic, has achieved synchronous broadcasting in 166 countries across the world. The audiences watching the live show at that night has transcended 20 million and the cumulative playing have been over 340 million times.

According to the *Report on 2016 China's Music Market Consumption* published by new media Rechord, 32% of interviewees choose to watch the live show of paid vocal concerts. The Chen Yuhua Mars Concert in 2016, broadcasted by LeMusic, is charged with 50 RMB for per performance. And there are over 130 thousand audiences choosing to pay and watch the live show of the two performances in Shanghai and Shenzhen.

According to the *39th China Internet Network Development State Statistic*, published by China Internet Network Information Center, the live shows of vocal concerts have developed its market in a speed next to that of game lives. Confronted with the fact that the resources with good quality is limited and the competition on copyright is intense, every broadcasting platform has given play to its advantages by enhancing the user experience, improving the payment business, developing offline business operation and strengthening business operations management. They work towards their goal of introducing users by superior content and realizing the viewings by multiple operations.For example, LeMusic has participated in the holding of Li Yuchun's 2016 Barbaric Growth vocal concerts. It has sent out coupons of Yongche, a platform providing renting and sharing car services, and membership card of LeSports, a website of exclusive broadcasting rights. This operation mode of combing selling and gifting has realized the increasing of values of online services by offline tickets. Bibi Chou's Boom!+ Beijing performance has launches a customized cellphone and if fans buy the cellphone, they will get tickets for the performance. The customized cellphone will send notifications of Bibi Chou's lossless music, exclusive information and news calendar and will also create customized rings of alarm clocks, etc.

1.2.1.3   Movie Festival

The year 2016 has seen 2100 vocal concerts and music festivals, increasing 10.53% than 2015. It has also witnessed a 9.69% annual increase of box office, reaching 3,488 million RMB in 2016.

There are more music festivals giving performances with higher frequency. After the transition in 2015, there are more than 500 music festivals being held in 2016, which has achieved a remarkable increase. Just take the example of the Strawberry Music Festival, it has been held in 22 cities across China. Except the overall growth of the number of performances, many music festivals have also been born in 2016, such as the Echo Music Festival, Valley Folk Festival and over 20 others. The reasons for the rapid growth of music festivals markets include: first, the overall development of the music industry, especially the promotion of originality and industrial shuffle benefited from the regulations of digital copyright, which makes live performancea vital way for music to create profits. Secondly, the enhancement of the commercial operation of music festivals has attracted capital to flow into this market. For example, the Echo has received 30 million US dollars from Beijing Enlight Media Co. in its series C funding, the Yema Livehas received tens of millions US dollars from Ming Capital in its series A funding, the Jungle Events has received tens of millions US dollars from Qingsong Fund and Legend Star in the angel round funding. The inflow of capital has propelled the expansion and update of music festivals. The third reason is that the successful holding of music festivals will prove the city's cultural competitiveness and will also become the city's name card. So music festivals have also received the support from the local government.

The market of music festival has gone into the process of vertical segments. The development of music festivals in each vertical segment is one of the remarkable features of the 2016 music festivals market. Those include electronic music festivals represented by INTRO Electronic Music Festival and MTA Music Festival, folk music festival represented by Valley Folk Festival and New Youth Folk Music Festival, jazz music festival represented by JZ Festival and Beishan Music Festival. The vertical development has made breakthrough for the stagnation of the homogenization of music festivals, which help it update to a new stage from "large and comprehensive" to "small but exquisite".

1.2.2 Dancing Performances

The year 2016 has witnessed 5900 dancing performances in professional theaters, which slightly increased than 2015. The box office of dancing performances reached 876 million RMB in 2016, which increased 5.04% than 2015. The market of dancing performances has developed in a relatively sluggish situation comparing to the rapid growth of concerts and stage plays in recent years.

Table 2-2 A Comparison between Dancing Performances´ Market in 2015 and 2016

Content	2015	2016	Percentage (%)
Performances (in 10,000)	0.59	0.59	1.72
Average Price (CNY)	125	140	↑
Attendance Rate (%)	44	41	↓
Number of Audiences(in 10,000)	235.14	231.36	-1.61
Box Offices (in million CNY)	8.34	8.76	5.04

1.2.2.1   China has well explored an overseas dancing market with close international cooperation.

Chinese dancing is an art with the highest commercial value in international market except acrobatics and martial arts for China. Ballet troupes, represented by the National Ballet of China and the Shanghai Ballet, and modern dancing troupes, represented by the Tao Dance Theater and Beijing Modern Dance Company, have given well performances during overseas commercial performing tours, which gradually established the popularity of the dancing troupes and the international influence of Chinese dancing. For example, the National Ballet of China has made a performing tour of *Peony Pavilion* staging for 13 times in the United Kingdom in 2016. It has created excellent box office and enjoyed high praise from British audiences. For another example, the Tao Dance Theater has been giving performing tours overseas for over half of each year and it attends 19 overseas art festivals in average every year.

The well performances of Chinese dancing in the international market is contributed from the objective fact that dancing does not meet language obstacles when performing and also it is less affected from cultural difference during expressing; The well performances is also contributed from the subjective situation that Chinese playwrights in first-class dancing troupes could create plays and design stage performances in international standard. The close international cooperation in creating plays has also broadened Chinese dancing troupes' views and created performing opportunities for Chinese dancing troupes to go on international stages. For example, the Liaoning Ballet has cooperated with the Johannesburg Ballet on the *Swan Lake* ballet performance. It has cooperated with Ivan, the chief director on the France's Rhine Ballet Theatre, of the modern ballet *Footprint*. It has cooperated with Swedish artist Mark on the modern ballet *Cliff Edge*. It has also cooperated with the famous Russian ballot dancer Grigorovich on performing the play *Spartacus, Romeo and Juliet*, etc.

1.2.2.2 The low acceptance of Chinese audiences inhibits the development of the market of dancing performances. So there is a need to cultivate audiences for dancing performances step by step.

Statistically, the number of audiences for dancing performances is presenting a falling trend. The language expressed by dancing requires people to be well versed in arts. The incapability of understanding builds the barrier between dancing performances and Chinese audiences. The lack of popularizing ballet causes the lack of audiences in China's market of dancing performances, thus the cultivation of audience for dancing performance needs hard work going deep step by step. The work includes at one side, strengthening the publication and education of dancing performances among teenagers, in order to cultivate audience for the future market; at the other side, the dancing troupes and theaters should base on the current evaluation level of audience to publish and promote their performances, so as to introduce the dancing performance from simple to hard.

Another reason for the sluggish development of dancing performance lies in the problem during innovation. Those innovations on Chinese dancing focus more on technique but less on connotation. And the homogenization among performances is widespread. If the dancing performance is lack of content, clumsy in expression, if the dancers only focus on the forms without any specialty, the dance will never be of good quality nor attractive enough to cultivate a stable group of audiences.

1.2.3   Theaters

1.2.3.1 Stage Plays

The year 2016 has witnessed 15,100 performances of stage plays, increasing 9.42% than 2015. It has witnessed the box office of stage plays given rise to 6.14% than 2015, reaching 2,437 million RMB in 2016. The stage plays has a widespread basis of audiences. The market of stage plays has also been stably developing in recent years. The weakness of innovation, however, is still one vital element that inhibits the development of China's stage plays. In order to make up those weaknesses, more importance should be attached to the innovation of dramatic texts and to the development of dramatic talents.

Table 2–3   A Comparison between the Stage Plays Market in 2015 and 2016

Content	2015	2016	Percentage (%)
Performances (in 10,000)	1.38	1.51	9.42
Average Price (CNY)	400	300	↓
Attendance Rate (%)	70	85	↑
Number of Audience (in 10,000)	284.03	320.88	12.97
Box Office (in hundreds of million)	22.96	24.37	6.14

The number of performances and income of stage plays have both risen and the falling of price has pushes up the attendance rate. In recent years, the stage plays market has shown a positive developmental trend. The scale of the stage plays market has been continuously increasing. The number of performance and box office of stage plays have both maintained a high growth rate in 2016. What is noteworthy is that the number of audience of stage plays has increased by a large margin in 2016, growing nearly 13% than 2015. But the average price has fallen sharply, which pushes up the attendance rate still further. The falling of stage plays price is benefited first from the subsidy from the government to encourage the public consumption on culture, second from the stage plays troupes' own choice of transferring some of the profits to audiences, in order to cultivate its market by low price and more performances, but not by high price and high income per performance.

The adapted plays are no lack of fine works. The weakness of innovation has driven stage plays to classic works. Many adapted plays made their debut in 2016, including those from Shakespeare, Tang Xianzu, Lao She, Henrik Johan Ibsen, Anton chekhov, Dürrenmatt Friedrich, Ding Xilin and other famous playwrights both home and abroad. For example, Chinese director Lin Zhaohua has directed three plays in 2016, which are *An Enemy of the People* from Henrik Johan Ibsen, *Dr. Godot or Six People Searching for the 18th Camel* from Dietrich Mateschitz and *A Midsummer Nights* Dream' from Shakespeare. For another example, the National Center for Performing Arts has adapted the *Leaning Tower of Pisa*, Beijing People's Art Theater the *Three Comedies by Ding Xilin* and Shanxi Province Xi'an People's Theater the *White Deer Plain*. Adapting the Chinese and foreign classic novels, movies, poems into stage plays is an insurance of the quality of the plays and box offices for stage troupes and directors.

The imported plays are diverse in styles and rich in different levels. The number of imported plays has been increasing annually from 2014. The International Theater Season from the National Center of Performing Arts, the Exquisite Plays Invitation Exhibition from Capital Theater, Lin Zhaohua Stage Dramas Invitation Exhibition, Beijing Fringe Festival, Wuzhen Theatre Festival and Beijing Nanluoguxiang Theater Festival have all become windows for China to get acknowledged of international theaters and platforms for matchmaking Chinese and international theater markets. They have also found their own niche when introducing plays, which brought up the situation that the imported plays are diverse in styles and rich in levels.

There are not only classic works from famous foreign directors acted by famous theater troupes, including Krysitan Lupa's *Hero's Square*, German director Thomas Ostermeier's *Richard III*, "Henry V" from the Royal Shakespeare Company, but also those small and experimental theaters such as French play *Cloture de L'amour*, Lithuanianplay *The Three Sisters* and *Madagascar*. What's more, innovative stage shows, which have also become a very popular art performance, have also come to perform in China, such as *Blue Man Group Show* from the United States, *Metropolitan* from Canada and *Stomp* from the United Kingdom.

1.2.3.2   Chinese Traditional Opera

Chinese traditional operas have been presented in professional theaters for 15,200 times in 2016, remaining almost the same as 2015. It has created box office of 864 million RMB, decreasing 6.78% than 2015. The declination of traditional opera's audiences has brought about the shrinking of this market.

Table 2–4　A Comparison between Chinese Traditional Opera's Markets in 2015 and 2016

Content	2015	2016	Percentage (%)
Performances (in 10,000)	1.52	1.52	-1.15
Average Prices (CNY)	200	300	↑
Attendance Rate (%)	74	70	↓
Number of Audiences (in 10,000)	342.43	319.20	-6.78
Box Office (in 100 million CNY)	8.94	8.64	-3.36

The performances from professional theaters polarized. Traditional operas have a more inclusive group of audiences, including Peking Opera,

Shaoxing opera, Henan Opera and Kunqu, develop, with the support of government, with a positive developmental trend in producing plays, giving performances, conserving the tradition and cultivating the audiences. For example, the *Four Dreams of LinChuan* published by Shanghai Kunju Opera Company has given 44 performances in its 2016 performing tour. And its 4 performances in Guangzhou Opera House have achieved over 90% of attendance rate with total box office reaching 1 million RMB. The *Phonix Hairpin and Butterfly Lovers* by Shaoxing Grand Theater have been performed in 46 cities in 82 performances, with over 80% of attendance rate in 2016.

The innovation in publication and marketing has expanded the market for traditional opera and cultivate their audiences. It includes plotting a fashionable theme in order to attract the young audiences, for example, melting the twelve constellations into the theme of the traditional opera highlights to make a thematic performing tour. It also includes using modern financial marketing to raise money by crowd funding through theatre goers. For example, the "2016 Wang Peiyu Peking Opera Oratorio in Nanjing" has received 85,038 RMB by 302 audiences through crowd funding, and in the end, the performance has achieved a great success. What's more, the innovation also includes using the modern technology to popularize traditional opera, for example, the small theater Peking Opera *A Feast in Spring* has used VR technology to film, so that audiences will feel at the scene when they watch the video.

However, most local operas and small theaters are facing the critical moment of surviving or perishing. Most of them are confronted with the situation of lack of finance, the break in the continuity of talents, shrink of market and the drain of market.

Village has become the fertile ground for opera performances. Under the influence of living customs and cultural consumption habits, opera performance has a huge market in villages. The recent years have witnessed a positive growing trend of traditional opera performances in villages. There are over 210,000 traditional operas held in Zhejiang Province every year, with around 15000 audiences watching it. Over 65% of the 520 villages afflicted with Yuanping city Shanxi province hold at least 7 traditional opera performances every year. The 1529 natural villages afflicted with Wuchuan City, Zhanjiang City, Guangdong Province, held over 3000 traditional opera performances per year, with special finance 25 million RMB and audiences nearly 5 million people.

The prosperity of the traditional opera in village is benefited from, at one side, the economic development in villages, which leads to the increase of cultural consumption. During occasions of spring festival, holidays or other important events such as marriage and funeral, traditional opera will usually get the opportunity of performing, which inherits and develops the tradition. On the other side, governmental policies also encourage performing arts troupes to perform in villages, in order to enrich the spiritual life of villagers.

Privately run performing arts troupes are the main resource to invigorate the traditional opera market in villages. For example, the Zhejiang Shengzhou Qunyi Shaoxing Opera Troupe has given over 600 performances in 2016, with performing income of 6.3 million RMB. Nearly 100 privately run Huangmei Opera troupes, in Huangmei County, Huanggang City, Hubei Province, have given almost 10 thousand performances in villages every year.

With the development of the market of opera performances in villages, intermediary institution, performing equipment, clothes production, stage construction, plot and publication, performing training and other relative industries have also grown up. The market of opera performances in villages has gradually matured its industrial chains.

1.2.3.3   Children's Drama

Children's drama has been shown in professional theaters for 20,600 times in 2016, increasing 10.16% than 2015. The box office from children's drama has been 966 million RMB in 2016, growing 7.81% than 2015.

Table 2–5   A Comparison of Children´s Drama´s Markets in 2015 and 2016

Content	2015	2016	Percentage (%)
Performances (in 10,000)	1.87	2.06	10.16
Average Price (CNY)	250	300	↑
Attendance Rate（%）	40	50	↑
Number of Audiences (in 10,000)	224.03	255.50	14.05
Box Office (in 100 million CNY)	8.96	9.66	7.81

The demand of children's play is thriving. In 2016, the audience for children's plays reached 2.555 million, increasing by 14.05% compared with 2015. The number of audience for children's plays increased for several reasons. Parents raise awareness of the importance of arts cultivation and educational role of plays. The increasing quality and various types of children's plays on the supply side have attracted more attentions of audience. Besides, the performance forms have varied. For instance, in 2016 more than 220 sessions of 40 performances in the Shanghai Children´s Art Theatre embraced play, music, dance and diversity, among which included modern dances, hand shadow shows and musicals.

With the adjustment of China's one-child policy, it can be predicted that the demand of children's plays will further bloom and that the family shows designed for parents and children together will be the favorite.

The number of imported children's plays mounted. Differences in creative concepts at home and abroad are prominent. Before 2015, it was rare to see imported children's plays in China's performing market. However, in recent years, the introduced children's plays have boosted in numbers and varied in types. Take the year of 2016 as an example, A.S.K.(The Art Space for Kids) has introduced 380 sessions of 15 foreign children's plays, including *We Dance Wee Groove* from the Multi-media Dance Journey by Stillmotion, UK, *Like Cat and Dog* from the Multimedia Interactive Theatre by Teatre Animal, Spain and *H2OMMES* from the Music Theatre with Live Animation and Installation by Adone, France. These introduced plays demonstrate the prominent features of close distance to the stage, more interactive and experiencing activities as well as breaking traditional relations between audience and performers. The goal is not only to tell a story or infuse knowledge through performance but also focus on cultivating children's practical and social ability, releasing one's nature and exploring one's potential.

We have witnessed innovations in China's children's plays over the course of past few years. Technologies like multimedia, 3D technology and virtual characters are introduced, but the content is still scenario-oriented. The lack of high quality original play is the major reason impeding the development of China's children's plays.

1.2.4　Chinese folk art and acrobatics performance

In 2016, the number of acrobatics performances in the professional theatres reached 8,700, which equals to the year of 2015. The box office earned more than 2015, totaled 928 million yuan.

Table 2-6　The Comparison of Acrobatics Performance Market in 2015 and 2016

Categories	2015	2016	Growth Rate (%)
Performances (in 10,000)	0.87	0.8690	-0.11
Average Price (CNY)	195	210	↑
Attendance（%）	41	40	↓
Number of Audience (in 10,000)	126.62	121.80	-3.81
Box Office (in 100 Million CNY)	9.16	9.28	1.31

1.2.4.1　The innovation of Chinese folk art expands the market.

The innovation of Chinese folk art not only interprets modern art via traditional Chinese folk art forms such as popular cartoon and storytelling adapted from online novels to attract young audience, but also innovate marketing model to invigorate traditional Chinese folk art. For instance, Shanghai Pingtan Troupe expands the market by crowd-funding, promoting financial products and issuing cartoon products. Apart from this, Benshan Media, Deyunshe and Hip-pop Bag Shop perform live shows on online platforms to explore more business opportunities.

1.2.4.2   The development of acrobatics hits a bottleneck.

The development of Chinese acrobatics in the domestic market remains slow and gentle. In the international market, however, it is warmly welcomed and favored. But in recent years, confronted with the international market saturation and market environment of intentional markdown and disordered competition, Chinese acrobatics groups are struggling for survival. Chinese acrobatics remains some concerns because they pay greatly attention to techniques but neglect art expressiveness. The challenging skill-flaunting performance that lacks of stories, fun and innovation can no longer meet audience's satisfaction nowadays. The major reason for bottleneck of Chinese's acrobatics development is that the model of talents training in Chinese acrobatics is traditional and outdated. Similarly, acrobatics actors also put great emphasis on skills cultivation but ignore the appreciation of art and culture, which causes the shrink in Chinese acrobatics talents exports to the international market. Besides, other reasons that cause brain drain in Chinese acrobatics include arduous training, short period of employment and low income. There is an urge to innovate the talent-training mode in Chinese acrobatics creation, adaption and performance.

1.2.5   Tourism performances and entertainment shows

1.2.5.1   Tourism performances

Tourism performances in 2016 reached 52,900 sessions and box office totaled 3.404 billion yuan, decreasing by 4.08% and 3.21% respectively compared with 2015. With two-year policy adjustment, the decline in tourism performance market slows down.

Brand projects enjoy a stable growth. Tourism performance projects such as Songcheng series, Landscape series and Impression series yield a steady growth. The revenue in 2016 grew more than 10%. The data of the Songcheng performances demonstrated that the growth of operating revenue and net profit doubled in 2016.

The rise of tourism performances is the result of scientific and rational decision-making in perspectives of project's location, investment control, performance creativity, art design, stage performance, costumes and props as well as tourist attractions arrangement. Therefore these projects will enjoy a longer business vitality and better performance.

Performances are not attractive with low audience conversion rate. According to the *Report on China's Tourism Development (2016)* from National Tourism Administration, China saw 4 billion domestic tourists in 2015 with 3.42 trillion yuan of tourism revenue. With the difference of growing tourists and revenue year on year, the audience and box office of tourism performances have witnessed a fall for years in a row.

The audience conversion rate (the audience conversion =audience of tourism performances in a city/ total number of tourists in a city) of China's tourism market remains at a low level. The rate is less than 4% in most cities (the rate in the US is 23%.). Even with more than 20% of conversion rate, tourism performance market in Lijiang is of little optimism. According to the 2016 annual report by the Tourism Development Committee of Lijiang, there were 750 performances of *the Impression Lijiang* with 1.5428 million tickets, decreasing by 23.64% year on year. The revenue reached 166 million yuan, dropped by 24.48%.

The Impression Lijiang is a typical case. Tourist groups takes up a great amount of proportion of *the Impression Lijiang*. With the growth of self-service traveling tourists, however, the drop of tourist groups does not make a contribution to the consumption of *the Impression Lijiang*, but lowering its growth instead. Meanwhile, their competition also disperses travel agencies' orders. With limited capacity within one area, confronted with competitions of the same consumption types and consumer groups, many performing programs have to bear the fall of business vitality. Given that people are prone to the new cultural performances than the old, the previous performing programs suffer great pressure with the emergence of new programs. The declining tourism performance and audience conversion rates mainly refer to the problems of monotonous plots, stereotype without creation and similar themes with less attraction. Many programs also bear the problems of lacking of preliminary planning and market assessment, following the suit blindly and producing shoddy products.

1.2.5.2   Entertainment shows

In 2016, performing theaters and groups staged 485,500 entertainment shows, an increase of 2.04% of 2015. The box office reached 2.455 billion yuan, a growth of 1.99% of 2015.

1.3   Performing theaters and groups optimize their arrangement.

The total revenue of performing theaters and groups in China was 20.705 billion yuan in 2016, growing by 5.58% of 19.611 billion yuan in 2015.

Table 2-7   The Comparison between the Composition of the Revenue of China´s Performing Theaters and Groups in the Year of 2015 and 2016

(in 100 million CNY, %)

Categories	2015	2016	Growth Rate
Government Subsidies	52.88	61.00	15.36
Corporate Sponsorship	2.50	2.27	-9.20
Commercial Performances	137.04	139.96	2.13
Performances Benefiting for the People	3.69	3.82	3.52
Total Revenue	196.11	207.05	5.58

In 2016, there were 87,900 performances in professional theatres, up to 4.52% compared with 2015. The total revenue was about 14.905 billion yuan, with an increase of 1.91% of 2015.

Table 2-8   The Comparison between the Composition of the Revenue of China´s Professional Theaters in the Year of 2015 and 2016

(in 100 million CNY, %)

Categories	2015	2016	Growth Rate
Sites Rental	42.12	40.06	-4.89
Self-Support Income	31.17	34.18	9.66
Property and Other Income	19.96	18.41	-7.77
Government Subsidies	53.00	56.40	6.41
Total Revenue	146.25	149.05	1.91

1.3.1 Modern management system for theatres and groups has been established gradually.

The performing theatres and groups have been striving to deepen internal reforms. With the application of modern technology, the level of management has been improved. With the improvement of incentive mechanism, the talent supporting has been strengthened. The establishment of modernization management system has further pressed ahead the transformation of performing theatres and groups to the market majority, enhancing the creativity and competitiveness.

For instance, Jingju Theatre Company of Beijing applies partnership approach. As the producer, theatres are only responsible for paying for publicity, plays producing and renting sites. The production team becomes shareholder with producing and rehearsal fees according to the technical levels and contributions and participates in box office profit sharing, which mobilizes team's creativity and responsibility.

In perspective of talents management, the Shanghai Dance Theatre pursues the system of "Professional Title", forming a ranking system with Chief, Solo A, Solo B, Lead A, Lead B and Group Dance. This system guarantees the advantage of talents training and leading effect but also expands and solidifies the basis of talents team. The Shanghai Ballet applies dual-track approach. On one hand, foreign talents are stationed as directors, instructors and guest dancers in China in order to create marvelous plays and dramas made by the Shanghai Ballet. On the other hand, star dancers are sent to the first-class international ballet groups for exchange and communication, making the talent structure of the Shanghai Ballet well-organized.

Many performing theatres and groups set up digital archives for the historical materials via information technology, keeping those precious materials in a longer storage, which will ensure that those archives can play a better role in spread and promotion.

1.3.2 Self-run performances in theatres increase. Status of industry is optimized.

In 2016, self-run performances in professional theatres and their revenue went up compared with 2015. On contrary, performances in the rented sites and revenue dropped. The proportion of the self-run performances increased from 42.57% in 2015 to 48.35% in 2016, which illustrates that theatre management has gotten rid of renting sites' low level management code step by step. Theatres optimize their industry structure, enhance performing and operating levels and form their own characteristics and brands by planning performing seasons, staging boutique repertoire exhibitions and participating in plays' creation. For instance, Tianjin Grand Theater that hosted the Tianjin Caoyu International Theater Festival caught people's eyes with high standard play shows at home and abroad. The Shanghai Cultural Square characterized by "professional musical theatres" experimented to produce self-made musical *the Spring Awakening*.

Table 2–9 The Comparisons of Performances and Revenue in Professional Theatres in the Year of 2015 and 2016

Categ ories	Performances (In 10,000)		Growth Rate (%)	Revenue (In 100 Million CNY)		Growth Rate (%)
	2015	2016		2015	2016	
Rented Sites	4.83	4.54	-6.00	42.12	40.06	-4.89
Self-run Sites	3.58	4.25	18.72	31.17	34.18	9.66

1.4　Performing arts agencies flourish.

In 2016, the revenue of all performing arts agencies in China saw 14.176 billion yuan, with an increase of 6.53% of 13.307 billion yuan in 2015 (Chart 2-5).

1.4.1　The IP–orientated copyright income boosts and the excessive entertainment structure emerges.

The copyright income from performing arts agencies has witnessed a consecutive growth for years in a row. In 2016, it was 1.329 billion yuan, increasing by 6.41% than last year. The value of copyright has been gradually explored and added. The IP is favored by capital. Some traditional performing arts agencies begin to leverage IP to develop in depth. For instance, Beijing

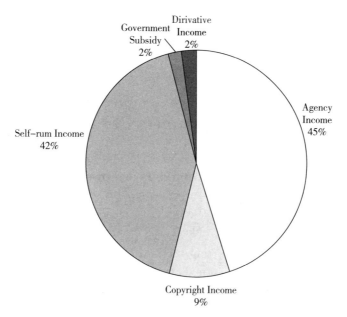

Chart 2-5   The Composition of Performing Arts Agencies´ Revenue in 2016

Century-Wonpennon Culture &Media Co. ,Ltd, the producer of plays of *the Li Lei and Han Meimei, the Go Away, Mr. Tumor,* and *the Forever Young,* based on the incubation and development of plays and dramas, deepen their structure in the field of cultural tour and play-film combination. Centering around diverse products with comedy elements, the Mahua FunAge further enhance commercial performance market shares and influence with its plays, musicals and children's plays. The superb IP products were adapted into online dramas and TV series, improving comedy talents incubation platform and related innovative business sector. The Songcheng performances set up extensive entertainment structure goals with performing arts, traveling, online performances, actor IP incubation, VR theme parks and overseas programs.

1.4.2   The niche artists´ performances and programs are co-operated in series.

Given that the niche market has less attraction to the mass and limited capacity to operate indie market, some agencies integrate resources together, providing professional teams and planning commercial programs. Take the

WANT U MUSIC by Juooo.com as an example. It is designed for small-and-medium pop music live shows. In 2016, the WANT U MUSIC witnessed 40 groups of artists' performances, including singers with popularity to some extent like Haomeimei, Chen Li, Ma Di. Damai.cn also launches music plan of "Mailive Solo Tour" with 20 groups of singers of different styles such as Wang Sulong, Xu Liang and Li Wei, in theatres accommodating thousands of audience as their initial tour.

1.5 Government transforms its supporting patterns.

The government has pressed ahead to change their way of supporting the market. Funds assistance, ticket subsidy and government purchasing cultural service replace supporting method of direct fiscal allocation. The goal is to change the fiscal supply with invigorating market majority vitality, cultivating audience, strengthening weakness and coordinating resources. The beneficiary will not only be the state-owned enterprises but private enterprises will also be included. The "cost-without-efficiency" supporting mechanism will be transformed to public bidding, assessment and performance appraisal. Apart from the China National Arts Fund, places like Beijing and Jiangsu establish provincial arts fund, playing a role in guiding and inspiring of arts development. The government policy supports and attaches great importance to the development of performing arts industry. The Ministry of Culture issued the *Thirteenth Five-Year Plan on Reforms of Cultural development*, aiming to introduce 50 representative plays and drams that stand for civilization of this era and the national culture image. In addition, artists will deliver lessons and training to 1000 persons. Government will give a hand to 100 plays' creation. All of these serve as significant indicators in the thirteenth five-year cultural development.

In perspective of government purchasing cultural service, the Ministry of Culture issued the *Management on the Ministry of Culture Purchasing Cultural Service from Social Force and Relative Directory Guidance*, incorporating public-interest performance into government purchasing list. The state-owned theatres and groups, especially those system-shift ones, will be able to participate in bidding and purchasing by offering performance services for approval. According to the *Opinion to Guide Government Purchases of Cultural Services from Society* issued by the Ministry of Culture and the Ministry of Finance as well as other two ministries in 2015, government should issue their own guidance out of their own circumstances, incorporating cultural performance into governments' purchasing lists. Moreover, many places also launched plans to purchase public-interest performances. The mechanism that "people-ordering, society –taking and government-paying" comes into being. For instance, there were 800 large-and-medium sized performances respectively in the public culture allocation program in the second half-year of 2016 in Shanghai. Shanxi province invested more than 11 million yuan in 2016 to purchase over 400 public performances within top eight theatres and groups, benefiting 400,000 people. Governments that purchase cultural performances services play a major role in nurturing the market by satisfying the mass's demand and enriching people's spiritual life.

People benefit from lower-price subsidy policy that will cultivate performance consumption habits and draw more attention into theatres. Take Tianjin as an example. Tianjin Bureau of Culture, Radio, Television and Tianjin Local Taxation Bureau have complemented and introduced *The Temporary Management of Special Funds in Supporting Refined Arts, Boutique Exhibitions and Public-interest Activities*. High-class performances introduced by Tianjin Grand Theater were granted with subsidies. Tianjin also issued "Cultural-Easy Cards" targeting 11 municipal state-owned theatres and groups. With government's subsidies of 400 yuan per card, citizens can get one that is worth of 500 yuan with only 100 yuan to enjoy the shows with discount from 30% to 80% off.

In terms of guiding cultural creation and nurturing performances market, it is remarkable that Beijing applies multiple and various methods. Arts funds support creation at the front end. Rehearsal centers guarantee security in the middle term. Theatres' service platform match needs with demands in the late period. Lower-price policy for the mass benefits the development of whole industrial structure at the terminal phase.

1.6   Performing arts develop with the Internet.

The Internet and performing arts co-develop in an accelerating speed. The "Internet +" brings changes in transmission, sales, profits and experiencing of performing industry.In return, performing arts provides content and consumers to the Internet platform. The webcast has already become the must in staging concerts, which will gain profit from copyright and online box office. Meanwhile, hundreds of times of growth of audience promote potential commercial value. For instance, the number of audience watching the Growing Wild—Li Yunchun's Tour in Beijing on the LeEco exceeded 5.66 million. In 2014, the number was only 48,000 in Wang Feng's concert. The peak of audience online in the Tencent of eye-catching Faye's Moments Live 2016 in Shanghai reached 21 million. In addition, with the spread and application of VR technology, the Internet brings fresh and new experience to the audience.

The Internet platform is not satisfied with only serving as broadcasters but begin to go offline. The LeEco, for example, hosted the MTA Festival and Li Yuchun's tour 2016. Ticket platform Gewara and 13-Month.com co-founded a corporate to provide all-round operational strategies for artists' records and tours.

Performing arts industry has been exploring online business. Shanghai Symphony Orchestra created online digital hall, enhancing R&D and application of online platform live shows and establishing platform for concerts. Director Stan Lai produced sitcom *the Rich House, Poor House*. The play was shot in the theatre. At the same time, the interactions with audience on the scene and advice from audience online were added in the production of the play.

1.7   The capital begins to flow into performing arts market.

China's performing arts industry as well as theatres and groups remain small in scale. Compared with other industries, it has higher risk in investment and financing system. However, with the improving performing arts market, the investment and financing system can be assessed and controlled. Performances have become a part of people's life. Based on the network of big cities, performing publicity and marketing have spread through the whole nation. The industry's structure has been optimized. The division in performing industry chain has been more and more specific. The industry speeds up to integrate, playing a prominent leading role. All of these advantages will give target and direction to the investment and financing system in China's performing arts market. Thus we can see the investment balance with proof. The ROI (return on investment) also rises. A series of growth in performing arts market such as copyright trading, interactive, open and interconnected ticket platform, digital stage design agencies for large-scale performances, online platform and marketing platform for products and services has become the investment hot spots. Some performing arts programs also draw attention of the investors like tourism performances with mass tourists and powerful marketing channels, commercial plays with national tours' opportunity and groups of audience, plays introduced from international classics with high recognition, cross-industry performing brands with attraction to consumption(like children's plays adapted from cartoon and animation) and comprehensive projects with combination of performances, training and entertainment.

1.7.1　The capital invests relatively slow into performing arts market.

On March 17th , 2014, the Ministry of Culture, the People's Bank of China and Ministry of Finance issued *the Notice on Matters concerning Promoting the Cultural and Financial Cooperation*, emphasizing on significance and opportunities on cultural and financial cooperation. It encourages the innovation on cultural and financial system, financial products and services that meet the demands of cultural industry development. It urges that the cooperation between two fields will guarantee the public service and financial support in cultural industry's investment and financing system. The performing arts market witnesses its opportunity to expand development with investment and finance.

In the second half of 2014, Yang Liping Cultural Media Group Limited was listed on New OTC(Over the Counter) Market, which marks that China has initiated the path of performing arts capital. Performing arts agencies expedited cooperation with capital market. According to incomplete statistics, dozens of performing arts agencies have been listed on New OTC successfully through capital operation. They are Hang Zhou Gold Coast Culture Development Co.Ltd, Beijing Century-Wonpennon Culture &Media Co.Ltd, Shandong Art Performance Group Limited, Xiamen Top-Sight Culture Media Inc., Beijing Fengshang Shiji Culture Media Co. Ltd, Henan Baihe Media Co. Ltd. and Hangzhou New Youth Troupe Co.Ltd. In March 2017, China's e-commerce giant Alibaba fully owned acquisition of China's largest online ticket platform Damai.cn, incorporating it into its culture and entertainment strategy. The capital also seeks for proper projects to invest. Chinese Culture Group Co. Ltd and Chinese Culture Industrial Investment Fund became shareholders of 48 Media that runs a large female idol group "SNH48". Juooo.com acquired hundreds millions of pre-IPO financing with Haitong Capital Co., Ltd. leading and Xiamen C&D Corporation Limited, Chord Capital and WENS following. Commercial Troupe JoyWay Drama gained tens millions of Angel Investment by HH Pictures Corporation Film. Compared with other sectors in the cultural industry, performing arts is the last one to be capitalized. In terms of capital market, performing arts theatres and groups that have monotonous content, could be influenced by non-market factors and are easy to be affected by market feedback of single product do not have enough strength. Therefore, capital should be cautious to enter into performing arts market.

1.7.2 Second–tier ticket platforms are favored by capital.

In recent years, several second-tier platforms were established and favored by capital. As the supplement of first-class ticket platform, playing a role of market adjuster, there is necessity for its existence and development. However, due to weakness in operation, management and supervision, those platforms have become the center of scalped even forged tickets. The lack of intervention mechanism to the premium tickets serves as the path for others to profiteer, disturbing market order and infringing consumers' rights and interests. Governments should introduce some regulations and strengthen supervision to cope with this issue.

Table 2–10   Parts of Second–tier Ticket Platforms´ Operation Code and Financing Details

Platform	Code	Establishment	Financing	Time of Financing
xishiqu.com	B2B2C C2B2C	The End of 2011	Millions of RMB from Pre-A Investment	January, 2013
			30 Million RMB from A Investment	October, 2014
			50 Million RMB from A+ Investment	January, 2016
tking.cn	B2B2C	July, 2015	Millions RMB from A Investment	October, 2016
			Tens Million RMB From A+ Investment	November, 2016
piao001.cn	B2B	December, 2015	Tens Million RMB from Angle Investment	June, 2016
uapiao.cn	C2C	2016	5 Million RMB from Angle Investment	June, 2016

Data Sources: China Association of Performing Arts, *2016 Year's Annual Report of China Performance Market.*

1.7.3   The resource of performance fund grows mature and crowd–funding becomes a highlight.

Thanks to the prospect of performing arts industry and its growing maturity in investment mechanism, more micro-and-small-sized performing enterprises start to focus on boutique production and large-sized cultural enterprises expand their potential. Especially the crowd-funding approach has grown into a trend in recent years. On one hand, people have access to high-end performances. On the other hand, niche and high-end performances could survive and earn reputation.

In 2016, popular crowd-funded Beijing Opera *the Prosperity Brought by the Dragon and the Phoenix* makes full use of the interests of young generation in online financing, combining the interests of cultural products and investors, integrating traditional operas and the Internet crowd-funding. With a brand new approach, it has declared the remarkable return of traditional cultural arts that have been known by more and more people. Cultural crowd-funding becomes a stepping-stone of expressing traditional culture in a new way. However, it should be noticed that though culture crowd-funding plays significant role in developing performing arts industry and raising vitality of cultural industry, most cultural products, especially traditional cultural products, still do not enjoy considerable competitive advantages in the face of developing difficulties after simple processing of the Internet. So we should deeply explore the combination of performing arts industry and crowd-funding as well as abundant qualified resources of funding.

The demand of entertainment grows so increasingly that China gradually enters the fast-developing stage of cultural entertainment consumption. Compared with international mature markets, China's domestic film market hasn't released its potential. It can be predicted that performances would draw more attention of capital. More performance agencies are willing to pursue new development through capital.

1.8 The integration of China´s performing arts market speeds up.

1.8.1 The main business expands diversely.

More and more major players in market begin to focus on advantageous business, developing diversely through the industry's chain and establishing industry's internal eco-system.

The management companies in the state-owned performing agencies reorganize its performing companies, transferring its performing business into original production. They try to set up ticket platform and learn about their memberships' demands, adjusting their business from single profit of theatre management and box office to multi-profits of ticket agents, performing organizations, copyright trading and online theatres. Some private performing theatres and groups form a "1+3" complete industrial chain featuring with performing management and combining performing production, tickets and theatre operation. The parent company serves as the major player while three subsidiaries are responsible for play's production, theatre management and ticket business respectively. As for ticket websites like Damai.cn, it heads to the offline operation by gaining the naming right of Dalian Sports Center. It strives to create smart sites in big cities, increasing commercial value and cooperation space in the fields of system, content and information application.

Some traditional performing agencies starts to organize their business in a extensive-entertainment way. For instance, YL Entertainment & Sports grows from a single ticket company to a comprehensive culture and entertainment enterprise. Now it has several business realms in ticket, film, performing arts, technology, sports, agency, 2D and public relation. The Songcheng performances set up extensive entertainment structure goals with performing arts, traveling, online performances, artist-oriented IP incubation, VR theme parks and overseas programs.

1.8.2　The cross–integration in performing arts market stands out.

On February 26th, 2014, the State Council issued *Notice on Matters concerning Promoting Integration of Cultural Creation and Design Services with Related Industries* to realize the achievement of promoting cultural connotation of tourism development as top priority. It was stated in the document that Chinese government support the development of tourism performances and products with regional and national characteristics. The accelerating integration of cultural industry speeds up. Performing arts integrate with films, tourism and other related industries, which brings vitality and broader development space to China's performing arts market.

The tourism performances have always been a very part of national performing arts market. Influenced by the *Tourism Law of the People's Republic of China* issued in October 2013, 2014 saw a drastic decline in tourism performances market. The reasons are as follows. Apart from several representative projects, most tourism performances have a lower level of production and are lack of original ideas and market attraction. After the cancellation of travel agency binding tourists' consumption, those projects can no longer survive. But it will impede the trend of integration of tourism and performing arts. In 2015, audience in tourism performances across China reached 47.13 million people, an increase of 31.2% than 2014. The number of plays and drams in 2015 was 95, declining by 28 performances. The 2015 box office earned 3.57 billion yuan, up 31.7% than 2014.

2. Characteristics of China's Performing Arts Market's Foreign Trade in 2016

In recent years, under the circumstance of global cultural industry and development of service trading, the mobility of competition factors of international performing market speed up. International performances and copyright trading is more and more frequent. With the influence of government's beneficial policies and improvement of regulations and service platform, relied on the sustained prosperity of the performing market, performing foreign trade enjoys a stable growth in the perspectives of numbers of plays, tours, audience and trade volumes. In 2016, the foreign trade enjoys a positive momentum in the fields of performing creation, performing mainstay's development, supporting policies and platform construction.

2.1 Performing arts markets share a closer tie.

In 2016, centering around markets in major cities, with the help of brilliant plays' tours, different markets move forward to an interconnected and comprehensive market in national scale. The basis of foreign trade lies in the highly prosperous domestic market. The very development of domestic market will trigger plays with high quality. With the assistance of domestic market revenue, we can balance the cost of performing products and service in international market where it can be more competitive. The constant spread and expansion of the first-class performing theatres and groups will be conducive to transmitting mature cultural resources and operation patterns to lower-tier cities in the initial phase. It will help shorten the gap of different markets and development and realize the united development in cultural market, thus enhancing the levels of performing arts industry and further laying a sound foundation for the export of performing products and services.

The domestic performing arts market is the basis of developing performing arts foreign trade and triggers performing products and services with high quality, which initiates the booming consumption demands and better understanding of the country's culture. It stands for our expression of cultural confidence and our endeavor on cross-culture and cross-era exchanges. Thanks to the development of cultural industry and market of countries within the Belt and Road, Chinese consumers' demands on performing arts industry flow into performing products and services of other countries and vice versa in return.

2.2 The import of performing arts industry propels its export.

2016's foreign trading market was still dominated by the introduced plays. But those plays were no longer performed without any changes. More and more performing theatres and groups made some adaptation and even participated in the process of production and creation. On one hand, they can adjust to the demands of Chinese audience. On the other hand, it is an effective way to deconstruct plays in details and learn about the experience of production and rehearsal. In that case, they can not only have insight in market's demand, but also press ahead development of their own creation and production.

At the same time, theatres and groups put great emphasis on the cooperation with international groups. From introduction and production to publicity and promotion, foreign teams imbue energy and vitality to China's theatres, which contributes to cultivating market-orientated and global ideas in production and performance. Take the *War Horse* conducted by the National Theatre of China and the National Theatre of the UK as an example. The Chinese version performed in the National Theatre of China had 58 performances, attracting 50,000 people. The average attendance was about 95%. This is a successful hit. The production of Chinese version learned from the experience of the National Theatre of the UK, such as cast choosing. The National Theatre of China applied public recruiting approach first time. This approach not only brings about talented people but also catches people's eyes. With a lot of investment, however, the price of the play is quite low, just one third of its counterparts. Its ticket company provides Chinese version's service in particular, altering the embarrassment of higher price and lower attendance in China's big-budget production. During the process of learning, Chinese teams absorbed and digested what they had learned. China International Venue Ally has been in charge of the *War Horse* in Asia independently and applied the UK's "whole-industry-chain" promotion pattern. Recently, Chinese teams will have cooperation with South Korean team for the Korean version, realizing our turn from "bringing in" to "going global".

2.3 Performances´ export goes up.

2.3.1 Increase in the export

In 2016, the income of preforming theatres and groups going abroad was 1.714 billion yuan, increasing by 4.42% than 2015.

The performances "going global" to the international market include some competitive Chinese acrobatics projects such as original acrobatics performances *Dream Trip* from Hu Nan Acrobatic Art Theatre which was staged 100 times in 70 cities of Canada and the US with 200,000 audience. Apart from this, there are also western arts performances of symphony and ballet such as 26 tours of the *Swan Lake* by Shanghai Ballet Troupe in Holland in 2016, 5 performances of the *Coppelia* in Montreal, Canada, 2 performances of the *Jane Eyre* in Bydgoszcz, Poland, 5 performances of the *Song of Everlasting Regret* in London, UK and original four-act ballet the *Butterfly Lovers* in Ottawa, Canada. In addition, Chinese traditional folk arts have realized achievement in the expansion of international market. For instance, the Yue Opera *Coriolanus and Du Liniang* by the Xiao Bai Hua Yue Opera Fund of Zhe Jiang Province has conducted performance in the UK, France, Germany and

Austria for 22 days.

With government support and business operation, "going global" thrives. On one hand, we can make Chinese culture worldwide, enhancing its influence worldwide. On the other hand, we can expand international market and be familiar with the market operation, establishing cooperation with foreign organizations and improving our operation capacity, thus fulfilling the transformation from "going global" to "selling global".

2.3.2 The export is dominated by play–output trading.

According to the International Exchange Bureau of the Ministry of Culture, the national acrobatics-orientated performing products of volume of foreign exchange reached 80%. China's performing export is dominated by acrobatics, Kungfu dramas and national stage plays. However, there is a shortage of musicals and operas. Acrpbatics and Kungfu dramas also suffer a shrink in international market. In the complicated international market, China's acrobatics teams always pursue interests in short term and sell plays to foreign theatres and groups in a long run, even signing actors directly to the foreign theatres as labor force output. This will not only lose copyright and derivative products' income but also lack of our own brands and influence. Cutthroats competitions among theatres and global economy inflict drastic decline on acrobatics and Kungfu dramas going abroad.

At the same time, China's theatres and enterprises still rely heavily on performing trading but copyright trading still does not come to the front stage. With performing trading, groups and enterprises can only obtain income within contracts but cannot gain more profits. More importantly, compared with copyright trading, performing trading is small in scale and has less impact on overseas market. Besides, theatres and groups' overseas projects put great emphasis on single performing programs but have few chances in cooperation and M&A with other theatres and groups.

2.4 Performing theatres and groups long for opportunities of "going global".

In the year of 2016, central and local theatres and groups actively conducted performances overseas and in Hong Kong, Macau and Taiwan regions with distinctive characteristics and abundant cultural resources. With the development of China's performing market, state-owned and private theatres and groups proactively participated in performance "going global". The service-trading platform is enhancing. The formation of performing trade transfers from traditional and single cross-border performance to multi-dimensional development of copyright trading, alliance agencies and joint venture production. More and more theatres and groups choose to head for international market and try their best to reduce dependence on government's support, making the market the source of development of theatres and groups and exploring a marketing pattern. For instance, Jingju Theatre Company of Beijing applies partnership approach to introduced *A Love Beyound*. In this open pattern, theatres only serve as the producer. Teams invest their income into projects so that the box office is directly linked with their income, which will greatly stimulate their initiative and enthusiasm. In terms of projects' marketing, it prefers to choose new methods for selling so that the span of audience will further be enlarged.

In 2016, China's performing market and international market cooperated in an all-rounded way and deepened integration in an open attitude. The international cooperation in the field of performing industry has deepened and expanded towards copyright trading and share investment. Cooperation among theatres and groups were deepened with more autonomy and diversity, including artists' cultivation, performance exchanges, plays' co-production and upgrade of management. Beijing Music Festival has signed a five-year cooperation plan with Aix-en-Provence Music Festival to further strengthen cooperation through education projects and public-interest projects. The Scenery Culture and Yue Guo Culture signed contracts of five live performances in Vietnam to interpret and explore its history and culture. Shanghai Oriental Art Center invested all the performances of the *Guys and Dolls* from the ATG. As for the copyright, the Sinocap bought copyright of Canadian play *Cavalia* and arranged 150 performances in Beijing.

Compared with the foreign performing trade in developed countries,

China's performing industry still has a long way to go in the perspectives of plays' creation, trade financing, insurance, international performing agencies and proxies, consultation on trade and law and trade regulation statisics. China should spare no efforts to shorten trade gap and enhance major theatres and group's international competitiveness.

2.5   Large-scale Cultural Exchange Programs Seeking Market Transition

With the marketization of performing arts, cultural trade has played an increasingly prominent role in cultural transmission, enjoying equal importance with cultural communication. Relying on the economic benefit brought by market operation, cultural trade is more sustainable than the exchange programs financially supported by the government. Against the backdrop of the great development of cultural industry and cultural trade prompted by the central government, performing theaters and groups that follow the mode of cultural communication have started to change, seeking social funds and promoting marketization of plays and operas. Particularly, large-scale cultural exchange programs such as comprehensive galas are endeavoring to achieve transition through business cooperation.

"Happy Chinese New Year" is a brand for large-scale comprehensive cultural activities founded by the government, with the aim to make the Spring Festival a well-known brand for Chinese culture's "going global". To date, "Happy Chinese New Year" has been held successfully for five years, becoming the largest activity of China's foreign cultural exchanges that combines resources from home and abroad, central and local governments, and state-owned and private enterprises. As a brilliant brand for Chinese culture's "going global", "Happy Chinese New Year" has launched various types of activities including parades on squares, temple fairs, artistic performances, galas on TV, book fairs and so on, providing a significant platform for China's cultural diplomacy, cultural communication, cultural trade and the improvement of China's soft power.

"Happy Chinese New Year" does not depend fully on the finance from the central government. Rather, it actively looks for partners globally for local cooperation. By effective measures and methods like building platforms, expanding channels and fund subsidies, "Happy Chinese New Year" has launched hundreds of high-quality commercial projects successively, accumulating great potentials for promoting international cultural trade and enhancing sustainability of its own. Meanwhile, with its increasing influence, more and more Chinese cultural enterprises and products regard it as an excellent platform to enter global market. The large-scale Chinese drama *Panda* invested by Jing Wen Record Company was unveiled in Las Vegas during the Spring Festival; the "2014 North America Happy Chinese New Year Chinese New Year Gala" organized by the Beauty Media Inc. in Los Angeles covered thousands of audiences. Marketization brings a win-win result for "Happy Chinese New Year" globally, benefiting both the spread of Spring Festival cultures and the "going global" of performing theaters and groups – the integration of performing theaters and groups rejuvenates "Happy Chinese New Year" in terms of both form and content. In return, "Happy Chinese New Year" offers a platform to excellent performing theaters and groups to go global.

2.6   Increasing Investment and Financing in the Copyright of Overseas Performing Arts

As China's economy cultural industry develop, investment and financing activities in the industry, especially overseas investment, have appeared not only in enterprises within the field of cultural industry but also in enterprises from other fields. The global economic slow down stands to be the good news for overseas investors to acquire or merge with some outstanding and high-quality enterprises with relatively low cost and risks. In particular, as a non-necessity, culture is likely to be the first choice to rid the market of bubbles during economic stagnation.

As for performing arts, a number of enterprises start to invest in the copyright of overseas performing arts, including the acquisition of theaters, buy out of the IP of plays and dramas, etc. On one hand, some investments go to the classical and mature dramas and plays in the western area of London and Broadway in the US. For instance, Juooo.com has started to purchase musical dramas of Broadway. On the other hand, several enterprises are not satisfied with investment, but desire to participate in the producing process of plays and dramas. With a long-term vision, these enterprises invest at the early stage of newly-created plays and dramas and track and support continuously, so that they can import the copyright to China in a better and fuller way. Ticketing agencies are a strong and active power in the market of performing arts. Based on their advantages such as the data analysis on their own platforms, ticketing agencies invest in stage plays, participate in the development of IP, and invest in and operate theaters. Take Yong Le Ticketing Agency as an example. "The Hunting Party – Linkin Park's Tour in China" became the first ever stadium-level tour of European and American rock bands in China, winning both reputation and box-office. Besides, Yong Le Ticketing Agency has opened branches in South Korea and other countries that have developed performing arts in an attempt to obtain high-quality contents and resources at the first opportunity.

2.7 Establishment of National Performing Arts Trade Service Platform

In 2014, the Ministry of Culture set up a public service platform for the establishment of a sound mechanism, the optimization of public services, the development of an international cultural and trade cooperation system, and the strategic construction of cultural markets at home and abroad, gradually forming a public service platform cored with performing arts, digital content, academic research and legal aid so as to, together with industry associations and research institutions, provide better public services for cultural enterprises to go global.

The Ministry of Culture commissioned China Association of Performing Arts to set up a "Exporting Service Platform for Performance Products", which targeted to assemble the export-oriented performing arts enterprises and projects, to strengthen cooperation with overseas industry associations, trade fairs and brokerage companies, and to gradually open up China's import and export channels for performance products. Also, the platform established an open and scientific selection mechanism for the export of performing arts to financially support demonstration projects selected across the country. Specifically, the Exporting Service Platform for Performance Products, in the aspect of information services, established an expert pool that gathers performing arts experts from home and abroad in the field of creative performances, production, and marketing, a domestic performance products pool that is classified by regions and equipped with supporting information services for export, and an overseas information pool that covers overseas performing places, brokerage firms and art festivals to help export enterprises of performance products expand their channels and sphere of cooperation; in the aspect of channel services, the platform provides informing about overseas performing arts exhibitions and various art festivals, promotes the rooting of international performing arts exhibition organizations in China, holds international marketing annual conferences for Chinese performance products, and builds an international promoting platform for Chinese performance products; in the aspect of personnel training, cooperating with the prestigious international art institutions, theaters and brokerage firms, the platform enhances the training of cultural trade to performers and brokers, and organizes senior staff in performing arts enterprises to study abroad in major art festival and performing agencies; in the aspect of promotion, the platform takes fully advantage of overseas embassies and consulates, cultural centers and media or new media to construct a multi-directional promoting platform for outstanding export-oriented performance products; at the same time, the platform sets up corresponding online service windows.

Meanwhile, the Ministry of Culture commissioned the Beijing International Studies University to take the lead to organize the China Institute for Cultural Trade Research (CICTR), with National Institute of Cultural Development (NICD) as the Secretariat. At present, the platform has cooperated with 35 universities and research institutions at home and abroad to directly better communication, coordination and cooperation among members as well as the organization of various activities at home and abroad. Besides, the platform serves experts on the platform to carry out theoretical and practice researches. CICTR is the convergence of domestic and foreign theories and practices on cultural trade. Based on the accurate grasp of the rules of international cultural trade, CICTR helps the structure adjustment of China's foreign trade, making use of academic research to promote the effective expansion of overseas cultural market, facilitate cultural enterprises to participate in practices of cultural trade, excavate and promote a number of classic cases of China's foreign cultural trade, and cultivate senior cultural management personnel with Chinese soul and international vision needed by the government. In such a manner, CICTR will gradually become an external think tank, a theoretical and practical research platform as well as a linkage platform for personnel training, serving national strategy. As an academic pioneer, CICTR provides related support, personnel protection and research services for the international development of China's performing arts.

In addition, the Ministry of Culture has also entrusted the China Cultural Industry Association to form a "National Digital Content Trade Service Platform", including the exchange of information, forums and conferences, exhibition and other traditional platform business with a further integration of "Internet +" to construct and operate an online platform. Taking advantage of the features of digital content products like standardization, digitalization and virtualization, the platform breaks the limit of time, space, software and payment with manufacture and trade as a breakthrough, realizing online production, remote management, online trade payments, online credit rating and other functions, and gradually promoting the copyright trade and investment trade so as to provide digital support and an Internet platform for cultural enterprises including the performing arts enterprises.

The establishment of the national platforms related to the foreign trade of performing arts is bound to cover the national performing arts market, so that the performing theaters and groups can achieve assistance in recognizing their own strengths and weaknesses, having access to the dynamic information of international performing arts market, understanding the channels for overseas performances, hiring and training personnel specialized in performing and management, etc. In this way, the foreign trade of performing arts will be more directional, organized and planned, being able to avoid, to a large extent, the high-added cost brought by opening up independently the international market by performing theaters and groups themselves.

2.8 Cultural Funds Promoting the Foreign Trade of Performing Arts

In 2014, the fund system began to be introduced into the cultural market, so that the state supports a more systematic, fair and reasonable management and uses of the funds for the development of cultural industry including the performing arts, thereby enhancing the vitality of the domestic performing arts market and easing the financial pressure of the foreign trade of performing arts. China National Arts Fund, established on December 30, 2013, is a social-oriented professional and public welfare fund established by the state, led by the government and reviewed by experts, covering nearly 80 kinds of art forms from tens of art categories including drama, music, dance, folk art, acrobatics, puppets, painting, calligraphy, photography and so on. It has become a new platform, channel and mechanism for the central government to manage, subsidize, support and guide the art industry for a healthy development. The establishment of China National Arts Fund is of great significance to the development of culture and arts. It is a concrete measure to promote the modernization of China's governance system and capacity. The fund is another achievement that reflects the institutional innovation of the Ministry of Culture with the transformation of functions, steering the creation and production of arts in an innovative way, promoting the separation of "management" and "regulation" in the governance of the art industry in China, and stimulating the cultural production of the whole society. China National Arts Fund has changed the mode of "directly supporting people" in the previous financial investment. Through the means of indirect sponsorship, expert review, social supervision and performance appraisal, China National Arts Fund has given full play of the guiding role of financial funds to not only ensure the openness, fairness, impartiality and transparency of capital investment and capital use, but also urge those who are supported strive to improve the efficiency of the use of funds.

In 2016, a total of 6,493 institutions and individuals applied for 7,248 projects to the China National Arts Fund, with the amount of funds totaling 7.51 billion yuan. Compared with 2015, the number of projects applied increased by 2,846, an increase of 64.7% to 2015 and 70% to 2014. In the projects, the number of stage art projects were 2,495, accounting for 34.4% of the total, including 1,106 large-scale stage plays and 1,389 small-scale stage plays/programs and works. Compared with 2015, the numbers increased by 285 and 600 respectively, or 34.7% and 76% respectively; 291 large-scale stage plays and works entered the second round of review, with 146 of them successfully being funded, an approval rate of 13.2%; 429 small-scale stage plays/programs and works entered the second round of review, with 159 of them successfully being funded, an approval rate of 11.4%. The 2016 Stage Art Funding Program no longer set up projects for major modifications and improvements of large-scale stage plays and works, which embodies the principles of originality and fundamentality

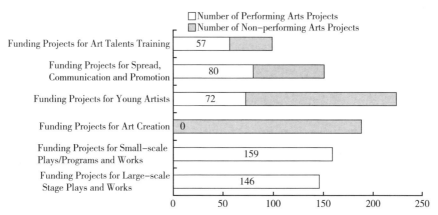

Chart 2-6　Distribution of Projects and Relevant Projects concerning Performing Arts Funded by the 2016 China National Arts Fund

and will make it a better "incubator" for the creation of new works, fully mobilizing the enthusiasm of creation. [1]

3. Urgent Problems to be Solved in the Foreign Trade of Performing Arts in China in 2016

3.1 Urgent Need to Establish a Systematic Statistical Evaluation System

At present, China's departments in charge of culture and China Association of Performing Arts are still in a non-standard state in terms of the statistics of performance data and performance trade. There is no real-time statistical system for performing arts among governments at all levels, so the statistical methods and standards of different annual reports of this industry vary, which also highlights the absence of supervision over foreign performance trade. The data released by China Association of Performing Arts is of higher accuracy and is the most commonly used annual data for the industry of performing arts across the country. However, the statistical indicators of China Association of Performing Arts only involve main and basic data, such as the number of performances, box office, ticket price and so on, without more systematic and detailed indicator design. Furthermore, since there is no universally-set statistical system and standard in China, the comparability of performing arts data from different provinces, cities or regions is low, obstructing severely trans-regional statistical analysis, and limiting or affecting the objectivity of the research and analysis concerning performing arts market. At the same time, the lack of a reasonable evaluation system for the regulative effect of policies supporting relevant performing arts, the effectiveness of national funds, the economic and social benefits achieved by performing theaters and groups will lead to a late feedback of performing arts policies. Besides, the government cannot supervise the

---

[1] Source of data: the official website and Wechat official account of China National Arts Fund

performing theaters and groups about the effect of preferential policies and the use of supporting funds by means of performance appraisal afterwards, so there is no restriction on them.

With the absence of a statistical evaluation system, whether the government, performing theaters and groups or organizations in this industry have difficulty in judging accurately the market size, play types, box office and social impact, and understanding comprehensively the current development of the national performing arts market. As a consequence, the anticipation of the future trend of performing arts market is affected, resulting in the lack of systematic support for government decision-making and a failure to control development direction for performing theaters and groups.

3.2   Lack of Excellent Performing Arts Brands and Passive Internationalization for Performing Theaters and Groups

Despite a continuous introduction of international plays, a surplus appeared in the foreign trade of performing arts in 2016. A short of internationally competitive plays and brands stands to be a key factor restricting the foreign trade of performing arts. There are many new plays in 2016 in the national performing arts market, some won a high box-office, producing certain brand effects. However, from the macro level, the national performing arts market still depends too much on star effect, and no performing theaters, groups or brands that have international influence and sustainable vitality stand out. Brand building not only depends on the creation of performing arts, but also is influenced by the management, promotion, marketing and many other aspects. Lack of operational funds, management imbalance, inaccurate positioning will hinder the emergence of performing arts brands. Lack of funds will not be able to support the entire industry chain, from creation, rehearsal to promotion and sales; lack of management will reduce the operating efficiency of the theater, increase operational risks, and even lead to a loss of excellent works and talents; if the market positioning is not accurate, it will be difficult to achieve an effective link between excellent performing plays and the demand of the market, resulting in a waste of resources. The international performing arts market has long been dominated by European and American countries, the main reason of which is that these countries have formed an international reputation as well as influential and high-quality performing arts brands. The most direct and effective way for China's performing theaters, groups and enterprises to compete with those mature ones in Europe and America is to create brands with sustainable vitality.

At present, the internationalization of the Chinese performing theaters and groups is mainly driven by the introduction of overseas plays, that is, indirectly driven by learning mature operational experience in the process of introducing overseas plays. Especially, theaters and groups will have a meticulous understanding about the creation, rehearsal, promotion and marketing of international classic plays through the introduction of copyright and localized adaptation. But compared to taking the initiative to participate in the international market competition, this passive internationalization is slow and lagging. Lack of excellent plays that can stand the test of the international market is the fundamental reason.

3.3　Imperfect Modern Enterprise System

The imperfection of modern enterprise system exists in various aspects for both state-owned and private performing theaters and groups. Enterprise-transformed state-owned theaters and groups have over staffing organizations, ambiguity of power and duties and inefficient management. Although by transforming to enterprises, the state-owned theaters and groups have been free from administrative units and established enterprise system, the interdependent and mutual-balanced corporation structure consisted by the shareholders' meeting, board of directors, board of supervisors and managers within the cultural enterprises is not perfect enough. The power and responsibility of leaders in theaters and groups are unclear. Therefore, there is either a lack of supervision and check for the "centralized" leadership, or a universality of too many internal frictions due to disputes. After transforming to enterprises, state-owned performing theaters and groups are still mostly invested by the central government and their property is simple and ambiguous, so many of them remain essentially in the model of "staffing of government affiliated institutions but managing as enterprises". A number of drawbacks of state-owned enterprises under the planned economy seriously remain in today's enterprise-transformed state-owned theaters and groups. Managers in these theaters and groups are mostly art workers, so their professional knowledge is relatively scarce and their management is relatively casual, which fail to be compatible with the corporation structure; meanwhile, there exists the situation that the selection of talents is not market-based − As the state-owned performing theaters and groups still rely mainly on state investment after transforming to enterprises, some specially-recruited staff of them are directly seconded to relevant departments in the government, resulting in additional costs of human resources.

Private performing theaters and groups are usually small-scale, so it is difficult for them to form a standardized corporation structure for governance. At present, many private performing theaters and groups are in their early stages of development, belonging to small-and-medium-sized enterprises or even small and micro-enterprises.Due to the single stock equity, the small scale, single products, simple management and other reasons, their management system combines investors and operators together and investors can operate and manage the enterprises directly. There is no need and conditions to separate the ownership and right of management for the enterprises. Thus, it is difficult to establish a mature and systematic corporation structure for governance.

3.4 Lack of Foreign−Oriented Management Personnel for Performing Arts

In 2015, the number of performing arts practitioners reached 348,612 (of which 301,878 were in performing groups and 46,734 were in performing theaters).The number of performing arts practitioners increased by nearly 37.75% in five years. China has a batch of national top theaters and groups, well-known performing artists at home and abroad, and world-class cultural brokerage firms. Also, a great number of universities in China are able to cultivate international talents. However, with so many outstanding performing artists and high-quality educational resources, the development of performing arts still lacks the support of creative talents and management personnel. The lack of creative talents for performing arts is mainly due to the absence of reasonable incentive mechanism and copyright protection mechanism, while the lack of management personnel, especially foreign-oriented ones, is due to the void of talent cultivation.

In the aspect of talent cultivation, compared with London, New York and other famous international metropolis for performing arts, the talent cultivation is disjointed with the application and practice of performing arts market in China. Many colleges and universities mainly concentrate on either the creation of works or the promotion and marketing of performance products when cultivating management personnel. Being too rigidly adhere to the theoretical research, these colleges and universities lack a clear understanding of the current development of the entire industry as well as an overall view of the whole industry chain, failing to make timely adjustments and reactions according to the demand of the performing arts market. Therefore, the supply of talents cannot respond to the demand of the market. It is increasingly urgent to train application-oriented, inter-disciplinary and foreign-oriented management personnel.

3.5 Imperfect Financing Environment for Performing Arts

In line with the *Notice on Matters concerning Promoting the Cultural and Financial Cooperation* published by the Ministry of Culture, Ministry of Finance and People's Bank of China in 2014,government departments and banks have implemented a series of measures to effectively exert the leveraging amplification effect of financial capital in an attempt to prompt cultural enterprises in the implementing process of cultural industry projects to use more financial tools to enhance their own market-oriented financing capacity. By the end of December 2015, the long-term loan balance in China's cultural, sports and entertainment industry totaled 245.8 billion yuan, an increase of 25.7%[1] year on year. However, the government's support is still unable to fully meet the demands of all the cultural enterprises, including those in the performing arts industry.

At present, the financing channels for small-and-medium-sized enterprises in the performing arts industry is not smooth due to internal and external reasons. First of all, the characteristics of the performing arts industry like high investment, unstable profit model, and too many uncontrollable factors, inability to reproduce rapidly as simple industries, and time-consuming creation in the early stage make it less attractive to the capital. In addition, China's performing arts industry is still in the initial stage of industrialization, so most of the assets in the industry are intangible like copyright and brand, which is difficult to handle for the traditional banking business. Moreover, there is an information asymmetry between the performing arts industry and financial sector due to the lack of financial knowledge in performing arts enterprises and the lack of understanding about the performing arts industry in financing institutions.

4. Advice for Promoting the Foreign Trade of China's Performing Arts

The long-term deficit in the foreign trade of China's performing arts reflects, on one hand, the strong cultural demands of the Chinese performing arts market on the other hand, the uneven quality of its own performance products and services. The performance products and services not only fail to meet the growing demand of the domestic performing arts market, but also cannot form influential brands in the international performing arts market to occupy the market share. The balance between supply and demand is the prerequisite for the healthy development of the performing arts market. The

---

[1] Data Resources: *Cultural and Financial Cooperation Made Breakthrough in 2015*, China Culture Daily, 2016-02-05,http://www.mcprc.gov.cn/whzx/whyw/201602/t20160205_460588. html.

long-term orientation of stimulating consumption to expand the demand side makes the gap between the supply and demand in the poor and weak market more and more obvious. The unsatisfied demand of performing arts thus transfers to the supply of international performance products and services, exacerbating the deficit in the foreign trade of China's performing arts. As China's economy develops into a new normal and the economic structure optimizes and upgrades continuously, the driving force of economic growth is shifting from factor-driven and investment-driven to innovation-driven. China's performing arts industry must also focus on improving the supply of cultural products and services to achieve the upgrading of supply structure in order to break the bottleneck of performing arts trade and create new opportunities for development.

4.1 Building World–Renowned Theaters and Groups with Chinese Characteristics

The construction of world-renowned theaters and groups with Chinese characteristics should adhere to the law of emphasizing the cultural heritage and national characteristics Chinese nation and respecting the development of arts and performing arts, the laws of the market, the flexible rule of culture exception when going global, and the principle of serving to satisfy people's cultural and spiritual needs.

4.1.1 Effective Connection between Policy and Market.

The policy-making for cultural development should be based on the effective connection with market to ensure that the supporting objective of the policy is single and clear and the policy serves the construction of a unified and open cultural market. Policies for the development of performing culture should pay attention to market demands, and supportive policies should be diversified, targeted and multi-channel.

4.1.2 Establishment of the National Honor System with Chinese Characteristics.

Establishing sound laws and regulations to protect the healthy operation of the national honor system on a system level. Adhering to the principle of openness and internationalization. Holding solemn and grand ceremonies on the National Day or in other important traditional festivals, with the head of state awarding medals to show the national-level attention and encouragement.

4.1.3 Exerting Effort to Build Diversified Market Entities.

Performing theaters and groups at different stages of development and with different characteristics should adjust themselves from the perspective of the market, business management, arts evaluation mechanism and so on to achieve the differentiated development. The use of single standard to evaluate the performances and management effects should be avoided. Diversified consumption needs for performing arts should be satisfied with diversified supply from the performing arts market. We should create a development environment in which a variety of performing arts enterprises are regarded equally and compete fairly, and promote the formation of an industrial pattern in which performing arts enterprises with different ownerships can develop commonly and large-, medium-, small- and micro-enterprises can help each other forward. We need to cultivate a batch of backbone theaters and groups with core competence, encourage various performing arts enterprises to merge with each other or reorganize themselves with capital as the bond, promote cross-regional, cross-industrial and cross-ownership merger and reorganization, and improve the scale, intensification and professionalization of the performing arts industry.

4.1.4 Enriching the Trade Pattern of Performance Products and Services.

To expand the scale of performing arts trade and enhance the international influence of performing arts should enrich and improve the trade pattern of performance products and services, achieving a common development of various patterns including the pure output, live performances, tour performances, copyright transactions and interaction with other industries.

4.2 Seeking Innovation for Mechanism of Theaters and Groups

Identifying some of the performing arts organizations as non-profit ones. Playing the supporting and guiding role of government in helping non-profit organizations with funding sources and tax incentives to ensure that these non-profit organizations can achieve their social value. The use of public cultural performing resources should focus on the equalization and sharing of resources among the market players, giving equal treatment to both state-owned performing arts enterprises and private performing arts enterprises, so that both of them can have healthy and free development as independent economic actors in the performing cultural market. In order to avoid repeated construction and a waste of cultural resources, an efficient and unified Integration Platform for Equipment and Resources of Performing Culture is needed to be established to promote the sharing of equipment and places of performing culture among regions. Perfecting the exit mechanism of the state-owned theaters and groups. Clarifying the different survival and development levels theaters and groups to cut down the number of theaters and groups that can barely survive. Integrating the theaters and groups with development prospects, and encouraging and supporting the development of independent profit-seeking theaters and groups to revitalize the performing arts market.

For theaters and groups that do not have the ability of "hematopoiesis", a set of exit mechanism should be established, which includes: improving the evaluation system and comprehensively assessing the operational capacity, cultural influence and development difficulty of the theaters and groups to set up an appraisal standard for the exit mechanism; improving disposable measures to theaters and groups and arranging appropriately exited theaters and groups or personnel by returning to administrative units, merging into other theaters and groups or dismissing directly to provide healthy channels for theaters and groups to exit the market. The establishment of the market exit mechanism, to a certain extent, can reduce the waste of performing resources and supporting funds, creating greater room and impetus for the development of advantaged theaters and groups.

Using policies to guide social forces to participate in the construction of public cultural services. On one hand, encouraging the government to invest in and subsidize copyrighted cultural products to be used free for public cultural services. On the other hand, adopting measures like the government procurement, project subsidies, targeted subsidies, loan discounts and tax relief to encourage all kinds of cultural enterprises and commercial cultural administrative units to participate in the construction of public cultural services.

4.3 Constructing a Scientific Statistical Evaluation System for Performing Theaters and Groups

Gradually abolishing the performance approval system and establishing thepost-regulatory system to combine a reasonable statistical index system and evaluation system with government funding and policy support in an attempt to force the theaters and groups to continuously improve their performance level.

First of all, we should establish a data platform for Chinese performing arts in time to know clearly the situation of the national performing resources, enterprises and market. We can learn from the weekly box-office system adopted by the Broadway League and set up platforms in performing arts market all over the country for data collecting and pilot monitoring. Besides, we can coordinate with cultural departments and statistical bureaus at different levels to gradually perfect the filing and data collecting system for the types, teams, office box and influence of performing arts that go abroad.

Followed by a scientific construction of regulation and performance appraisal system, performing arts enterprises will be truly guided into the market to compete with international and domestic counterparts. Scientific and rational design of the index system will make the regulatory and evaluation indicators closely related to creation, production, marketing and many other links to avoid assessing the performance of domestic performing theaters and groups simply based on the size and number of performances, so as to promote the formation of a comprehensive and sound market-oriented management system for national performing theaters and groups. According to the evaluation system, the government can commission the professional third-party social organizations to conduct an open, fair and impartial assessment. After the establishment of a mature index system, the government can authorize China Association of Performing Arts and other professional organizations and institutions in the industry to collect data and assess the performance of the theaters and groups. Organizations and institutions within the industry should be given the right to decide objectives and the use of preferential policies and funds such as arts funds, financial aid, editing the list of important export-oriented cultural enterprises and so on according to the assessment results with unified distribution and management. Considering the market factor, we should link the performance of theaters and groups with incentive policies. The statistical evaluation system assessed by a third party can not only guarantee and continuity and authenticity of data but also stimulate theaters and groups to focus on the quality of performance and market efficiency.

Meanwhile, we should further improve the appraisal method, improving the practicality, objectivity and efficiency of appraisal and supervision by means of organizing experts and consumers to participate in the inspection and appraisal, conducting social researches, publishing assessment results, inviting media to supervise, etc.

4.4 Boosting Trade of Performing Arts with Countries along B&R

Countries along "the Belt and Road" should be the prime partners of foreign performing arts trade with China since they are located closely to China and have similar culture and history with China. The initiative of "B&R" builds not only the road of economy and trade, but also the bridge of culture and friendship. Considering the different economic development levels of countries along "B&R", the performing arts trade between China and other countries must be conducted in an orderly way according to the maturity of their respective performing arts market and region. During the past decade, the import demand for cultural services has increased rapidly in central and eastern European countries, with the import volume of cultural services totaling $6.7 billion in 2012. However, the cultural services from China occupied less than $100 million. The politics and economy in central and eastern European countries are relatively stable and their culture market is as mature as China's. Geographically, central and eastern European countries function as a hub linking Asia and Europe. In addition, the "16+1" cooperative mechanism between China and central and eastern European countries will serve as a significant "port" for the integration of "B&R" Initiative into European economic world, prime targeted regions for the four partnerships between China and Europe as well as the new growth pole of China-Europe cooperation. Central and eastern Europe will be the first hinterland for China's foreign trade of performing arts. In the future, China's foreign trade of performing arts should continue to step into other mature cultural markets in Europe and America geographically. Based on the maintenance of market share, China should develop intensively emerging cultural markets in Southeast Asia and India, exploring actively latent cultural markets, especially those in central and eastern European countries.

4.5 "Going Global" of Performing Theaters and Groups to Help Cultural Exchange

Cultural trade is the most extensive cultural exchange. In recent years, cultural exchanges have been criticized for disrupting the normal law of the cultural market. Cultural exchanges and cultural trade are both important means to promote the spread of Chinese culture overseas and to enhance the impact of Chinese culture. On one hand, it is unsustainable if we neglect the role of market and blindly rely on cultural exchanges. On the other hand, some performing theaters and groups with weak capital and small profit margins cannot bear the cost of overseas promotion by depending on independent market-oriented operation and, thus, cannot export excellent plays to the international performing arts market. Therefore, performing theaters and groups should make good use of the overseas channels and promotion platforms brought by cultural exchanges to fully understand the international performing arts market in order to pave the way for their international business. By the end of 2016, China has established 30 Chinese cultural centers overseas, and the figure will continue to expand in the future. The space available of the overseas cultural centers and the effective use of the latest information on the local market can greatly save the cost of performing theaters and groups for venue rental, channel acquisition and market research when promoting overseas. Overseas centers can form a fixed mechanism and brand to introduce outstanding performance products and services to the local, which not only enriches the functions of overseas cultural centers, but also expands promoting channels for performing plays.

Cultural exchange and cultural trade complement each other, and the government guidance cannot replace business entities. Cultural exchanges must clear the way for the cultural trade and should never disrupt the market, interfere with the market and even undermine the market. The performing theaters and groups should cultivate the idea of promoting cultural trade through cultural exchanges in the process of participating in cultural exchange activities every year, and begin to take advantage of the opportunities of overseas cultural exchanges to investigate the international performing arts market, display excellent plays and seek suitable foreign partners.

4.6　Optimizing the Investment and Financing System for Performing Arts Industry

The performing arts industry in China is still at the early stage of industrialization, with small-and-medium-sized enterprises as the main actors. From the reality, the investment and financing system for China's performing arts industry should be more a top-down design.

First of all, we should deal with the relationship between performing arts business and performing arts industry properly, promoting a coordinated development between the two. Performing arts business should be motivated to, within its ability, collaboratively innovate with performing arts industry in terms of the training of performing talents, the sharing of creations, and the cooperation of performing venues and promotions, realizing a common development of both. Government's support to the performing arts industry should be more reflected in the optimization of financing environment, rather than direct financial supports. Because the government's financial resources are limited, so the financial funds should be used as a lever to generate more social funds. By establishing the platform, the government can promote the investment of more social resources, and improve the efficiency of management to performing arts industry with the help of non-governmental organizations, such as the China Association of Performing Arts. These non-governmental industries have more experience and understanding of specific issues within the industry, such as the industrial characteristics, development trends and competitive landscape. We should speed up the construction of the investment and financing system for performing arts industry and promote the relevant departments to implement policies and measures that encourage and guide the social capital into the performing arts industry to provide sustainable power for the development of performing arts industry. We should further expand the field and scope of social investment and motivate social capital to go into the performing arts-related business incubators, maker spaces, protection and development of cultural resources and other emerging areas. We should deepen the cultural and financial cooperation, give full play the coordinated effect of fiscal policy, financial policy and industrial policy to provide financial support for the entry of social capital into performing arts industry. We should implement policies such as "Awards in place of subsidies" and "Fund Injection" and support and guide social capital to flow into performing arts industry with the promotion of cooperative pattern between government and social capital in the industry as the handle. We should take advantage of the national investment policies, incorporating performing arts industry into the supporting range of investment policy instruments.

In addition, the government should speed up financial innovation to improve the investment and financing varieties and to build a strong alliance of performing arts enterprises, solving the problem of asymmetric information in the process of investing and financing from both vertical and horizontal perspectives. The online financial platform also provides opportunities for the financing innovation in the performing arts industry.

The concept of "crowd-funding" is a result of the application of group buying and pre-order models to investment and financing. Many small businesses, artists, or individuals, using the crowd-funding platforms, present their creative ideas to the public and at the same time raise the funds needed to start the project. Crowd-funding offers possibilities of achieving goals to small businesses and individuals who have passions for creation.

4.7 Improving the Talents Training Mechanism for Performing Arts Creation and International Operation and Management

Due to decades of rigid educational system in China, the traditional narrow definition of performing arts talents as performing talents by cultural management departments, the barriers between different disciplines, lack of communication and cooperation between arts academies and ordinary universities in terms of talents training, and the shortage of discussion and research on interdisciplinary talents training, China is now desperately lacking talents for creation and operation and management in the process of seeking internationalization and marketization, and a great number of performing talents are facing some embarrassing situations like job transferring, being laid off or retiring in advance because of the genres of their performance. Therefore, it is urgent to construct a perfect talents training mechanism for performing arts, encouraging collaborative innovation and common development and cultivating qualified personnel urgently needed in the performing arts market, so as to promote the sound development of performing arts enterprises and market. We need to continue to strengthen the cultivation of creative talents, especially the export-oriented and interdisciplinary senior management personnel, to establish a linkage mechanism for professional talents majored in cultural trade based in universities and directed by market. We should actively encourage and support the establishment of cultural trade majors in colleges and universities, guiding them to focus on professional courses, set up a curriculum with their respective characteristics, firmly grasp the core of economics, and form unique styles for this major; we should take advantage of university resources to lay a solid foundation for professional development; we should adhere to the school-running model that combines teaching and research to create an open and professional curriculum; at the same time, we should improve the quality of talents training through scientific research projects and establish the platform that promotes the cooperative cultivating model for cultural trade talents by using political, industrial, academic and research resources. Attention should be given to the strengthening of practice courses in order to give full play to the role of teaching practice bases, realizing a seamless linkage between campus education and practices in performing arts industry with comprehensive forms including internship in enterprises. With application-oriented cultivation and international vision as the target, we should promote the training of professional talents and strive to cultivate all-round talents who are familiar with domestic and foreign performing arts markets as well as foreign performing arts trade.

In 2016, national-level specialized service platforms shifted from establishment to maturity, which, coupled with the strong support of the China National Arts Fund, provided new opportunities for the development of China's performing arts market in many aspects including the policy environment and financial support. Meanwhile, problems that had been neglected for a long time such as statistical evaluation system were becoming increasingly obvious. Overall, the development of China's performing arts market has entered a stabilized period. The steadily growing market stood to be a prerequisite for a smooth development of the export of performing arts. With optimized market structure and supporting policies, the smoothly-developing performing arts market in China will definitely usher in a new growth point.

Part III Appendix

Appendix I Academic Synthesis of National Cultural Development

1. Brief Introduction

National Institute of Cultural Development was co-founded in 2010 by Beijing International Studies University and the Ministry of Culture's panel on culture system reform. It is a research institute for theory and practice on international cultural trade including public cultural cause and industry, cultural exchange and trade and cultural heritage development. Centering around National Institute of Cultural Development, China Institute for Cultural Trade Research, Beijing Research Institute of Cultural Trade, Beijing Collaborative Innovation Center for International Cultural Trade and Cultural Exchange and International Research Center Jingju Heritage were established in succession. Thus the international and comprehensive synthesis of academic service came into being. The National Institute of Cultural Development serves as the secretariat.

For the purpose of meeting international strategy of the national culture development, Beijing International Studies University has initiated the research on theories and practice of cultural trade since 2003, which fully exerts the unique role of academic diplomacy, and has become a explorer and architect of theory on cultural undertakings of China and international cooperation between China and foreign countries, an academic pioneer of research practice, an advisor and promoter of governments' decisions' consultation, a director of innovative cultivation of talents, an escort of the inheritance and development of cultural heritage and an advocate and provider of industrial trade promotion.

The synthesis of academic service undertakes projects authorized by governments at all levels. Many academic achievements accomplished have been adopted to promote the policies and measures of cultural trade directly. In addition, it provides academic support for deepening reform of the cultural system through projects at the national level and teases out cultural policies and regulations of various countries to promoting the regulation of Chinese cultural management. The synthesis of academic service is known as the "academic institution with craftsman spirit". Especially Beijing Research Institute of Cultural Trade focuses on the international strategy of Beijng culture development. It was selected by the first batch of Chinese Think Tank Index(CTTI) at the end of 2016 with characteristic of the research of cultural trade.

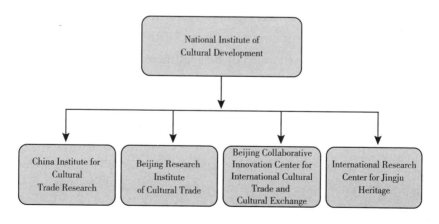

Chart 3–1   Schematic Diagram of Academic Synthesis of National Cultural

China Institute for Cultural Trade Research is authorized by the Bureau for External Cultural Relations, Ministry of Culture and headed by Beijing International Studies University, being established in 2014 with cooperation with 33 domestic universities and institutes and 17 foreign organizations, such as Communication University of China, University of International Business and Economics, Central University of Finance and Economics, Shanghai University of International Business and Economics, Chinese Academy of International Trade and Economic Cooperation, MOFCOM and Intertrade in China as well as Newcastle University, Columbia College Chicago, KOCCA overseas, Hungarian National Trading House and the Research Center for National Cultural Development Strategy of Serbia. The establishment of the Institute promotes the collection of resources of the cultural field at home and abroad, the innovative research on theory and practice of cultural trade, the cross-border trade in cultural products and services, the compound talent cultivation of cultural trade and the effective development of cultural market overseas.

Beijing Research Institute of Cultural Trade is a research base of philosophical-social science in Beijing characterized by theory and practice study on international cultural trade, mainly about four dimensions on theories of international trade, capital foreign cultural trade strategies, development of Beijing culture international market and expansion of foreign trade and cultural enterprises' cross-border operation and international development.

Beijing Collaborative Innovation Center for International Cultural Trade and Cultural Exchange was headed by Beijing International Studies University, under the guidance of the Ministry of Culture and the Ministry of Commerce. The Center was co-founded by colleges, institutes and organizations including CCPIT Beijing, Jingju Theatre Company of Beijing and Communication University of China. The center pursues serving capital culture and developing international strategy as major targets, talents training as core, discipline as basis and scientific study as support, constructing "Talent-Discipline-R&D" development code, directing towards accomplishment of tasks and goals of national cultural development international strategy.

International Research Center for Jingju Heritage was established by National Institute of Cultural Development and Jingju Theatre Company of Beijing. Well-known Jingju artist Mei Baojiu was its honorary director. Under the guidance and support of Mr. Mei, the center is committed to conveying traditional art in a modern way. Through Jingju's branding, marketing and internationalized developing both markets at home and abroad will promote Jingju's development and spread.

2. Main Work Contents and Results

2.1 Explorer and Architect of Theory on "Culture Going Global"

Closely integrating with the international strategy of China's culture development,studies on theory and practice of cultural trade were inaugurated in 2003. Efficient research teams were organized. In the spirit of "pragmatism" promoting "politics, production, study and research", they have conducted theoretical and practical studies in several perspectives in cultural field.

2.2 Pioneer of "Culture Going Global"

As the carrier of "culture going global", cultural products and services are easier to be accepted by foreigners. The recognition towards academic ideas and views suggests that Chinese culture is adapted in more areas, and showing more far-reaching influence Also it represents the value of the academic diplomacy. Bearing the role of "academic diplomacy" with willingness and autonomy, academic institutes cooperate with other sides in, upholding the spirit of "equal dialogue and confident expression". They precisely meet the demands of industry's trade with academic concerns as their foothold. In the process of broadening dialogue channel, constructing conversation mechanism and fighting for academic voice, they strive to overcome all difficulties and challenges, making contributions to "culture going global".

2.3　Advisor and Promoter of Governments´ Decisions

Oriented from the think tank of global cultural development strategy, research institutes broaden their horizon with multilevel-target study, supporting international strategy of China's cultural development with information and intellectual resources. Over the course of the past decades, with years of valuable and abundant study achievement, they provided suggestions for governments, pressing ahead introduction of policies and measures related to cultural trade. Studies on the reasonable application of policies were issued. The achievement helped State Council's *Notice of Matters concerning Cultural Trade Development* in March 2014. It made contributions to development of cultural trade and promoting export of cultural productions and services, aiming at promotion of cultural trade projects authorized by the Ministry of Commerce, Ministry of Culture and State Administration of Cultural Heritage. Besides, projects could be applied via National Planning Office of Philosophy and Social Science and Beijing Planning Office of Philosophy and Social Science, including subjects of cultural trade, cultural trade development code, international cultural trade path, culture "going global" policy and cultural market.

2.4　Director of Innovative Cultivation of Talents

In 2003, Beijing International Studies University started the course Studies on Hotspots of International Cultural Trade with following-up research in theories and practices of international cultural trade, which was the first among similar Chinese universities. A large number of international and comprehensive management talents are needed because of the rapid growth of cultural industry and cultural trade. To respond to the trend, BISU began to enroll bachelor students on International Economy and Trade(International Cultural Trade) in 2007. In 2009, the major of International Cultural Trade started to enroll under the approval of the Ministry of Education; And BISU was granted to issue Master degree on International Cultural Trade in 2012; in 2016, the University started to educate post doctor on international cultural trade. Thus, a multi-level education system on the talents of international cultural trade was formed.

2.4.1   Establishment of Cross–subject Master Project on International Cultural Trade

The cross-subject master on international trade has enrolled students speaking different languages and from different majors, such as economics, management, foreign language and literature. It is the goal to educate internationalized and comprehensive talents who have understandings on the theory and practice of international cultural trade, and international trade rules, practices, policies and regulations. They should also have global vision and speak foreign language, academic and innovative research ability, and participate in cultural trade. The resources on China Institute for Cultural Trade Research enable the formation of tutors group from universities and enterprises to cultivate needed talents.

2.4.2   Co–education Model that Leads the World

The co-education of Bachelor and Bachelor-Master program for international cultural trade talents under the cooperation with universities from UK, US and Australia can pool the resources of universities and educational institutes and make innovation on education model. The "1+3" Bachelor program and "3+2" Bachelor-Master program break through traditional education model, form an international platform for the education of comprehensive talents.

2.4.3   Education with Policy Makers, Industry Participants, Scholars and Researchers

To establish an education and research team government, industries, universities, research institutes and practice system, to hire experts in cultural trade as tutors and to form a tutor group with academic and language tutors, we have signed strategic cooperation agreement with tens outstanding companies in international cultural trade, including Perfect World (Beijing) Internet Tech Co., Ltd., Beijing Gehua Culture Development Group, Lion & Phoenix Culture (Beijing) Co., Ltd., Huayi Brothers and Shijibo Culture Development Co., Ltd. Education bases were set up with these companies, and "Perfect World Scholarship" on cultural trade was created, providing long-term mechanism for talents cultivation.

2.4.4   A New Normal for the Education of Cultural Trade Talents

We have promoted the integration of academic studies with scientific research and practice, established an "Eagles Plan" for students self management based on research projects and frontier practice in order to encourage students to participate in scientific research and academic service under the guidance of experts, providing systematical channels for cultural trade research and practice, assisting the development of students.

2.5   Escorting the Inheritance and Development of Cultural Heritage

The research team attaches equal importance to cultural trade and exchanges, is committed to the coordinated development of cultural industry and cultural affairs, serves the development of culture through cultural trade research projects, and achieves the internationalization, protection and inheritance of culture. With the target of promoting the brand "Beijing Jingju" and to make Jingju Theatre Company of Beijing a world-class theatre, we wish to inherit, develop and internationalize "Beijing Jingju", laying a foundation for the "going out" the traditional Chinese culture.

2.5.1   Co−establishment of "International Research Center for Jingju Heritage"

On March 26th 2012, the International Research Center for Jingju Heritage was established by National Institute of Cultural Development and Jingju Theatre Company of Beijing. Mr. Mei Baojiu, famous Jingju artist, and Mr. Han Yongjin, chairing head of Policy and Laws Department of the Ministry of Culture, were honorary directors, Mr. Li Enjie, chairman of Jingju Theatre, and Prof. Li Jiashan, Executive Dean of National Institute of Cultural Development, were directors in charge of implementing research results.

2.5.2   Clarifying the English Translation of Jingju, Setting up a Brand for International Cultural Trade

Jingju has been translated into "Beijing Opera" for long, confused it with western operas. After discussions and researched of some Jingju artists, linguistics, translators, cultural experts and economists, the literal translation of Jingju can convey the essence of the content and character of the Chinese culture, highlight the charm and influence of Jingju as art in international communication. In the business shows of Jingju Theatre, the name "Jingju" was accepted by international audience, setting up the brand and laying a foundation for international performance market.

2.5.3 Compiling One Hundred Classics in Different Languages for Inheritance and Promotion

When *Beijing Jingju 100 Stories Synopsis Standard Version (Chinese-English)* was compiles, it was hard to tell classic Jingju stories in a simple way and to suit the reading habit of Chinese and international readers. It was accurately translated into different languages to promote Beijing Jingju. Both 32 cuttings and pocket versions are available to meet readers' habit. It took 15 months for the compilation with 15 drafts and 5 times proof reading. After the official publication in September 2013, other 5 versions (Chinese-German, Chinese-Japanese, Chinese-Spanish, Chinese-Portuguese and Chinese-Korean) were published.

2.5.4 Establishing Platform for Cultural inheritance and for international promotion of Jingju

During "China-UK Creative and Cultural Trade Forum 2015", Mr. Mei Baojiu visited Britain and delivered keynote speech on "the Contribution of Mei Lanfang's Performing Arts to the World", exerting profound international academic influence. It was the first time after Mr. Mei Lanfang's performance in 1935 that Mei Baojiu introduces the contribution of Mei Lanfang Jingju performance system (one of the three major performance systems in the world) to world drama arts.

2.5.5 Organizing High-end Forum for the Expansion of Jingju Market at Home and Abroad

Since the establishment of the research center, five "Jingju Inheritance and Development International Forum"were held. The forum invited representatives from the government, universities and research institutes to contribute their wisdom to the branding of "Beijing Jingju" and its "going out". The results of academic studies gave rise to activities including "The Trip of Singing" , "The Trip of Inheritance" and Review of the Road of Mei Lanfang global performances by Beijing Jingju Theatre.

2.6 The Advocate and Provider of Industrial Trade Promotion

Creative theories and precise experience is conducted for industrial trade through systematic and persistent academic research. By holding institutional activities, academic institutes build up an interaction dialogue platform for specialists from production, study and practice, and an academic platform, including annual forums like "International Cultural Trade Forum", "International Service Trade Forum" and "Culture Restructuring and Chinese Cultural 'Going Abroad' Forum".

2.6.1 Establishment of Trust Platform for Cultural Enterprises

The overseas access is connected with cultural enterprises through sponsorship and participation of human-to-human exchanges. So far, it has co-staged "creative industry and cultural trade forum" with partners including the UK, South Korea and Australia so as to gather cultural enterprises home and abroad, study related topics, share cut-edge developing experiences, provide connectivity for domestic and overseas cultural enterprises, realize effective match for supply and demand. Cultural organizations contribute to international cooperative projects through the international cooperative institutes of academic study platform connected with overseas partnership, including Jingju Theater Company of Beijing, Warner Bros, Imaschina, TFF advanced custom jewelry brand, Beijing Quju Opera Troupe, China Association of Performing Arts, China Educational Channels, which effectively promote cartoon film cooperation between China and Hungary, copyright business between China and Romania for overseas trade of cultural enterprises and organizations.

2.6.2 Provider of Intellectual Training for Cultural Enterprises

It actively promotes employee training of cultural trade which benefits the people engaging in management, overseas trade and cultural exchanges in government and cultural enterprises, and directly involves in national cultural trade training hosted by the Ministry of Culture and the Ministry of Commerce. It offers cultural trade training for different regions like Beijing, Qinghai Province, Henan province and Nanjing, and for organizations like Beijing Performance and Art Group and China Association of Performing Arts. It successfully hosts "China-Holland human-to-human exchange", during which specialists from Van Gogh Museum and Reinwardt Academy launched museum exhibitions and talent training for relic protection. Also it involves in China-French Exhibitor Training. It offered specific training for social organizations like China Association of Performing Arts and Beijing Branch of CCPIT for cultural enterprises like Beijing Performance and Art Group.

3. To the Future

The strategic goals of the National Institute of Cultural Development is to serve as the foreign intellectual pool of national cultural development, the information think tank of global cultural development strategy, theoretical study plateau of international cultural trade, intellectual training base of international cultural management. The institute will commit to promote globalization and commercialization of cultural industry and the process of international cultural trade academic research.

Appendix II China Association of Performing Arts

1. Introduction

China Association of Performing Arts, a primary social group affiliated to the Ministry of Culture, is an organization of self-discipline for performance units and performers. It was established in 1988 as China Academy of performance managers and was renamed as China Association of performers. In 2012, an approval was issued by the Ministry of Civil Affairs to set its name as China Association of Performing Arts.

The Association has corporate members including performing troupes, venues, companies, agencies, ticketing companies, and stage engineering companies, and individual members such as brokers, actors, screenwriters and directors. There are 28 provincial-level performing associations in China, with around 10 thousand members and branches like Theatre Committee, Drama Committee, Children's Play Committee, Music Drama Committee, arts Education and Promotion Committee, Stage Engineering Companies Alliance, Agents Alliance and Online Performance (live) Association.

China Association of Performing Arts follows the principle of serving members and the industry, provides services including: compiling The Annual Report on China's Performing Market; compiling industry standard; carrying out self-discipline and investigation activities; providing consulting service on policies to safeguard to legitimate rights; qualification for agents and other industry participants; organizing China's Fair on International Performances, Annual Meeting on the International Sales of China's Cultural Products, Promotion and Transaction Fair on National Arts Troupe; establishing industry credit evaluation system; establishing public service platforms for the export of performance and arts products; promoting international cultural exchanges and performance projects; promoting the development of performing industry in a standardized, professional and international direction.

2. The branches of China Association of Performing Arts

2.1 Theatre committee

The Theatre Committee of China Association of Performing Arts is consisted of professional theatres, playhouses, concert halls, arts centers, and conference halls. Under the guidance of the Association, guided by the core values of socialism, the Committee sets self-discipline standard, unites members, adheres to integrity, upholds the legitimate rights of members, promotes their coordination and solves their differences in hope to prosper the performing market and to advance the establishment of socialist spiritual civilization by adhering to the Constitution, laws and regulations.

The Committee engages in business including: carrying out investigation in theatres, providing advices to departments in charge, promoting policy support for industry development; formulating self-discipline regulations, safeguarding the legitimate rights of members, providing legal consultant service, protecting the proper interest of the industry for healthy development; organizing exchanges between members, and business, skill trainings to better equip theatre management personnel; advancing communication with performance groups, agents and related fields, innovating operational methods for sound development; coordinating market demand and resource allocation for equivalent development; establishing contacts with major theatres, arts festivals, fairs and performance institutions from the world, and organizing members to participate in international academic and business exchanges.

2.2 Drama Committee for Small Theatres

The Drama Committee for Small Theatres of China Association of

Performing Arts is consisted of group and individual members engaging in drama creation, production, performance, operation, promotion, education, training and theatre management as well as other industries related to the prosperity of drama. Under the guidance of the Association, following the important thoughts of General Secretary Xi Jinping in arts symposium, based on socialism values that pursue the true, the good and the beautiful, the Committee formulates self-discipline regulations for small-theatre dramas and promotes the standardization of fields relating to small-theatre drama.

The Committee engages in business including: strengthening exchanges on drama creation, promoting the cooperation between drama creation and theatre performance, innovating the operation of small theatres for sound development; establishing self-discipline mechanism, standardizing hardware conditions and service, promoting the development in producing, performance, operation and management, safeguarding the legitimate rights of members; coordinating market demand and resources, establishing platform for performances, development and communication between regional small theatres for the prosperity of small-theatre drama in different regions; strengthening the contacts with world major drama festivals, establishing a mechanism to help "Chinese culture going abroad", setting up a communication platform for international drama through "going out, inviting in" policy; organizing business and skill exchanges, combining talents cultivation in practice with classroom education to support the creation, production, operation and management in the future; investigating in small theatres to identify problems of development and providing advices to departments in charge for a healthy development.

2.3 Music Drama Committee

The Music Drama Committee of China Association of Performing Arts is consisted of group and individual members engaging in music drama creation, production, performance, operation, promotion, education, training and theatre management. Under the guidance of the Association, following the important thoughts of General Secretary Xi Jinping in arts symposium, based on socialism values that pursue the true, the good and the beautiful, the Committee formulates self-discipline regulations for music drama industry. It unites members, adheres to integrity, upholds the legitimate rights of members, promotes their coordination and solves their differences in hope to prosper the performing market and to advance the establishment of socialist spiritual civilization.

The Committee engages in business including: strengthening exchanges on original creation, promoting the communication between producing units and theatres, innovating the operation of small theatres for sound development; coordinating market demand and resources, establishing platform for performances, development and communication for its prosperity in the market; strengthening the contacts with world major music drama festivals, exhibitions and academic exchanges by setting up an international platform for communication; organizing business and skill exchanges among its members, combining talents cultivation in practice with focused education; investigating in the industry to timely find problems in development, collecting advices from the whole industrial chain and hand in advices to departments in charge; applying for policy support for healthy growth; establishing a trusted media platform where investors can receive professional guidance, establishing an investment platform to inject more capital into the market.

2.4   Agents Alliance

The Agents Alliance of China Association of Performing Arts is consisted of group and individual members engaging in actor agents. Under the guidance of the Association, following the important thoughts of General Secretary Xi Jinping in arts symposium, based on socialism values that pursue the true, the good and the beautiful, the Committee formulates self-discipline regulations for actor agents. It unites members, adheres to integrity, upholds the legitimate rights of members, promotes their coordination and solves their differences in hope to prosper the performing market and to advance the establishment of socialist spiritual civilization by adhering to the Constitution, laws and regulations.

The Alliance engages in business including: strengthening exchanges between agents and other performing institutes; establishing self-discipline mechanism, standardizing the management and service, promoting the development in promoting, planning, operation and management, safeguarding the legitimate rights of members; coordinating market demand and resources, establishing platform for agents for their prosperous development in China; organizing business, skill and information exchanges among its members, combining agents education in practice with focused education; investigating in the industry to timely find problems in development, providing advices to departments in charge; organizing annual meeting for agents, expanding the influence of the Alliance in the market; providing third party consulting service and performance guarantee service to members.

2.5　Online Performance (live) Association

The Online Performance (live) Association of China Association of Performing Arts was established under the guidance of the Market Department of the Ministry of Culture. It is consisted of live broadcasting Internet platforms and agents for on-line anchors. The aim of the Association is to establish the ecology of online broadcasting and performance, to improve the quality of on-line performance and to standardize the industry.

The Association engages in business including: organizing cooperation for online broadcasting platform, online anchor agents, offline performing institutes and other related industries for greater space of development; organizing trainings to improve the quality of industry participants; establishing a platform for the exchanges among members and information sharing in order to promote sound competition and common development; investigating in the industry to timely find problems in development, providing advices to departments in charge; organizing annual meetings, awarding, promoting and expanding the influence of the Association in society.

Appendix Ⅲ　National Digital Content Trade Service Platform

Established on Jun 29th, 2013, China Cultural Industry Association is a national social organization approved by the State Council and registered by the Ministry of Civil Affairs. Members are consisted of outstanding domestic cultural enterprises and public institutions, covering such cultural areas as performing arts and entertainment, forums and activities, internet culture, cartoons and games, movie and TV media, crafts and arts, cultural tourism, cultural finance and e-commerce. Since its establishment, China Cultural Industry Association has been committed to building high-level platforms for international exchanges and devoted to education and charity. Meanwhile, it actively develops cultural trade and international exchanges to promote Chinese culture to "go global". China Cultural Industry Association also participates in and organizes international exhibitions and guides international merger and investment.

"National Digital Content Trade Service Platform" is a public service platform led by China Cultural Industry Association, which includes the exchange of information, forums and conferences, exhibition and other traditional platform business with a further integration of "Internet +" to construct and operate an online platform. Taking advantage of the features of digital content products like standardization, digitalization and virtualization, the platform breaks the limit of time, space, software and payment with production and trade as a breakthrough, realizing online production, remote management, online trade payments, online credit rating and other functions, and gradually promoting the copyright trade and investment trade. Besides, the platform encourages national digital content enterprises to take part in international trade actively, breaks barriers of trade information and technology, responds to the concept of "mass entrepreneurship" advocated by the government, makes up for the technological and industrial blanks in the field of digital content trade service, realizing the growth of foreign cultural trade.

1. The Status of the Platform in the Industry

Established in 2016, Ci Shiyun Co., Ltd. is confirmed to be the core operators of "National Digital Content Trade Service Platform" owing to its introduction of innovative technology, internet and thoughts. Led by the Ministry of Culture and organized by China Cultural Industry Association, National Digital Content Trade Service Platform, or "Ci Shiyun Platform", is the only national platform that covers the whole field of digital content. With "the third party, marketization and internationalization" as the target, the platform introduces the "Internet +" mode into the field of digital content, forming a digital content trade ecology that subverts traditions thoroughly and constructing a complete industrial chain for service trade – setting up flexible and customized individual production pattern, multi-person and multi-region task crowdsourcing production pattern, long-distance directors interactive pattern and virtualized communicative demonstration pattern. While helping enterprises complete quickly domestic and foreign digital projects, the platform can optimize cost and efficiency.

The platform follows the standardized procedure of digital content service: high-end and stable equipment + efficient and advanced technology + scientific and reasonable standards. The core competence of it is "standard and service". By setting up online task distribution mechanism based on the remote collaboration system on the cloud, deepening the digital content service industry and expanding outsourcing sectors of digital service, the platform has become a bond linking out sourcers and servers.

2. Functions of the Platform:

By innovating outsourcing production pattern with the help of Internet and launching new digital supervision service, the platform improves greatly the efficiency and convenience of the production of digital content;

According to the security standard of MPAA and Disney, the platform constructs initiatively remote cloud production system, guaranteeing the security of digital assets and intellectual properties to the largest extent;

By automatic filtering and cost performance recommendation, the platform can reduce the cost in medium- and final-period;

The company constructs itself a world-class virtual studio to offer independently-developed systematic solutions and real-time preview services.

3. Advantages of the Platform

3.1 Mature Application Platform for "Online Cloud Services"

Currently, platforms for digital services in the world only provide online register, information matching, remittance from the third-party agencies and other basic services. There are no management of projects and subprojects, no proceduress or steps for the confirmation and feedback of projects and no standards recognized by domestic counterparts. With complete and independent intellectual property, the platform can provide perfect solutions and services for B2B large-scale digital service projects, realizing user's remote control over the complete procedure of the project: online real-time confirming all project procedures, allowing the nested logic in projects and subprojects, allowing rollback and cycle of projects, and allowing many people to produce online remotely. This is also the only workstation-level digital service cloud platform in the market, including functional systems like task distribution, coordinated comments, cloud-linked payment and digital production. Key steps and procedures are as follows.

3.1.1 Project Liaison between both Sides of Production

From the home page, users can view recommended projects, know more about projects they are interested in, communicate with the first party, bid and eventually undertake the project.

3.1.2　Funds Settlement Procedure

Both two sides can communicate, negotiate, submit tasks and make suggestions for revision with the task list. The system will, according to the task list, task period, task time and other information, automatically complete steps of locking funds, payment and information record, so that both sides of production will only focus on the progress of the task while other complicated steps will be managed by the system automatically.

3.1.3　Production

The system will provide a unique confirming system. Every submission, revision and confirmation should be confirmed by users and recorded by the system for later check. Only necessary cyclical funds will be frozen. Documents of the project will be encrypted by the system so as to safeguard rights and interests of both sides.

3.2　New Digital Supervision System

Transforming traditional production system, the platform aims to create a global digital supervision system based on Internet. By introducing the concept of project supervision into digital production, interactive confirmation, payment, digital property protection and remote desktop control will be achieved in the procedure. The platform plays the role of supervisor, recorder and protector of rights and interests in the process, ensuring digital security and covering all key procedures of the production.

100% security of digital property. Allowing remote check of digital property, which permit both sides to check 100% digital details while protecting digital security.

Covering 95% of the production procedure. Except the part of sign and signature, all other production procedures (95%) can be controlled and completed online.

Improving 60% of efficiency to confirm documents. The efficiency to confirm steps in the production procedure will be improved by 60%, and all documents to be confirmed will be stored on the cloud for later check.

New field of digital production. By making it convenient for producers to follow up the progress or even the procedure of production through the Internet, the work efficiency has been improved by 80%.

3.3   Funds Ensuring and Digital Property Management Mechanism Cored with Security

The platform boasts secure standard to protect technologies and pays attention to improving core competence by intellectual property protection. The running third-party transaction system and digital property management system are consistent with the complete realization of the international security standard of MPAA and Disney: transaction security, coordination security, virtualization security and mobility security.

3.4   IP Incubation Mechanism Cored with the Value Preservation and Increase of Creative Ideas

Early demonstration is the key part to attract investors. At present, there are a number of excellent plays in China confronted with problems like the lack of attractive demos or the lack of funds for the team. To selected IP creative works, the company plans to use international industrial resources and backgrounds including low-cost but international team, advanced equipment and outstanding production pattern to promote the growth of the cultural creative industry and undertake the production of demos, preserving and increasing the value of creative ideas.

4. Major Achievements of the Platform

In 2016, the transaction volume on the platform reached 11.88 million yuan. The platform helped with the completion of 6 large-scale projects of Hollywood and Disney. The number of registered businesses was 108 and 700 practitioners were trained on the platform. The number of people who used the platform totaled 7300 for the whole year. The company researched and developed independently 15 platform application systems and relevant technologies, acquired 7 software copyrights, applied 8 patents and registered

1 trademark. Representing the province of Tian Jin, the company participated in the 12th China International Cartoon and Animation Festival and the 11th Beijing International Cultural & Creative Industry Expo.

4.1 Project of 4K Digital Film Repair

The platform has had a complete procedure of technical solutions to the repair of 4K digital films and been responsible for the repair of digital films of hundreds of old movies in Hollywood. As the only domestic repair team that can meet the international standard, the platform is the long-term and deep cooperative partner of MTI Film from the United States and China Film Archive. Representative projects of the company are *Heidi, Transatlantic, The Front Page, The Mating Call, The Horse Thief, Yellow Earth*, etc. The company offers service to many enterprises including the MTI Film from the United States, China Film Archive, and Three Dimension Six Degree (Beijing) Polytron Technologies Inc.

4.2 Projects of Cartoons and Animations

Projects of cartoons and animations mainly focus on the adjustment and rendering of cartoons. From July on, the company has achieved a transaction amount of 4.4 million yuan. The representative project is *The Arabian Nights*. The company offers service to many enterprises including Beijing Hebei Cultural Media Co., Ltd. and He Shan Film (Tian Jin) Co., Ltd.

4.3 Projects of Special Effects

The platform provides all digital post-services such as DIT, VFX, color matching and transcoding, with a transaction amount of 4.1 million yuan. Representative projects are *If the Prince Falls Asleep* and *Finding Soul*. The company offers service to many enterprises including The Walt Disney Studios (China) Inc. and Vision Square Special Effects Inc (Tai Wan).

4.4 Projects of Digital Production

The platform initiatively construct a digital production system based on the Internet, with cooperative users and partners paying attention to and supporting. During the trial operation, the transaction volume reached 3.28 million yuan.

Postscript

Research on the Situation of System Reform and Development Path of State Performance Art Troupes is a key project of National Social Science Foundation in Arts (code: 13ZD05, referred to as the project hereafter). The project was chaired by Prof. Li Xiaomu, Deputy Dean of Beijing International Studies University (BISU), reviewed by Leading Group Office of the National Arts Science Program and concluded in March, 2018. Thanks to the efforts by all parties, especially National Institute of Cultural Development and project team members, the project achieved important research result, and is to exert academic influence after its conclusion.

Research on the Situation of System Reform and Development Path of State Performance Art Troupes, with its basis of China's status as a big developing country, provides comprehensive research on the reform of China's performing art troupes under the deepening reform of cultural system, and discusses possible academic direction. The project offers better knowledge on the management, development, internationalization, marketization and rule-based improvement of arts troupes. With an insight on the economic, managerial and cultural rules for the reform of troupes, it serves as a boost to the research of cultural reform and innovative development, and to the application of cross-field theories. This practice-oriented project helps national level troupes with their problems in reform after all-round research, providing valuable reference for the decision making of government and enterprises. The research process follows the rules of cultural products and services, focuses on theoretical problems on art troupes' reform, and carries out systematic studies on the reform, upgrading the research in this regard to a new height.

The project was divided into five sub-projects: Prof. Li Jiashan of

BISU was the head of *Research on Reform and Evaluation System of National Performing Arts Troupes*; Lu Juan, researcher with Central Academy of Cultural Administration (CACA), was the head of *Innovative Research on the Reform of Performing Arts Management System*; Bi Xulong, researcher of CACA, was the head of *Innovative Research on the Development of National Performing Arts Troupes*; Prof. Wang Haiwen of BISU was the head of *Research on the Internationalization Strategy of National Performing Arts Troupes*; Xu Shipi, former researcher with China ACG Group was the head of *Research on Cultivating and Improving China's Performing Arts Market*. Prof. Li Xiaomu, along with his team, engaged in in-depth analysis on the reform of national performing arts troupes, with evaluation system, management, development mechanism, market and internationalization strategies as key. Special importance was attached to field trips. The team joined the researched on cultural system by the Ministry of Culture, sent 500 persons to basic-level troupes, collected 200 samples of troupes' reform, wrote 40 study reports, formed Data Collection and Analysis System of National Performing Arts Troupes which then became an intellectual property.

Under the project, the team submitted several reports on practical problems, many of which were adopted by former Ministry of Culture and related organizations in Beijing, leveraging the consulting values of the project. *Performing Arts Cooperation Serves the Belt and Road Strategy* was collected into *Culture Think Tank Report* of former Ministry of Culture; *Further Deepening the reform of National Troupes in Beijing* (No.0830) by PPC of Beijing won "2015 Outstanding Proposal of Beijing PPC"; research results including *Research on Running and Managing Performing Arts Troupes in German-speaking Countries* and *Research and Analysis on Overseas Market for Performing Arts* were adopted by the Leading Group Office of Cultural System Reform; *Russia Drama Culture Market and Policy Analysis* and *Economic Analysis on China's Ticket Prices of Performing Arts* were published on *Culture Decision Making Reference* by former Ministry of Culture. Other research results include 7 academic paper such as *The Export of Performing Arts: the Uniqueness and Trend of Trade Mark*; 5 books such as *Capital Cultural Trade Development Report 2015*, *Research on the Development Path with Chinese Characteristics*, *Observation on Cultural Reform Practices* and *Research on World Famous Troupes: Reform and Innovation*; series books of *Beijing Jingju*

One Hundred Classic Synopsis Translation Version in 6 transcript versions: Chinese-English, Chinese-German, Chinese-Japanese, Chinese-Korean, Chinese-Spanish and Chinese-Portuguese. The results received sound feedbacks in decision making, research, theoretical discussions, data analysis and team building.

The research team on international cultural trade from BISU makes up the core of the project. Under the cooperation with CACA, over 20 experts on economics, management science, arts studies, philosophy, Chinese language and literature, foreign languages and literature, and over 30 experts from politics, industries, universities and research fields formed a team that was scientifically structured and energetic. Under the support of National Institute for Cultural Trade Research and Beijing Research Institute of Cultural Trade, the project has incubated 2 national level research projects, 2 social science projects of the Ministry of Education, 8 provincial level research projects, 15 local level research projects, and engaged 50 persons in international exchanges and cooperation, exerting lasting influence.

The office for chief expert and the secretariat of the project is located in National Institute of Cultural Development. They followed the rules of National Major Project of National Social Science Foundation in Arts, organized academic studies, promoted cooperation, with effective communication, gaining experience for high-level projects management and service.

Market Development Report of Chinese Performing Arts (Chinese and English Version) is one of the results of the project, worked out by the team and China Association of Performing Arts.

National Major Project of National Social Science Foundation in Arts
Research on the Situation of System Reform and Development Path of
State Performance Art Troupes,
Chief Expert Office
Secretariat
May, 2018

图书在版编目(CIP)数据

中国演艺市场发展报告 / 李小牧，朱克宁主编. --
北京：社会科学文献出版社，2018.5
ISBN 978-7-5201-2661-8

Ⅰ.①中… Ⅱ.①李… ②朱… Ⅲ.①表演艺术 - 文
化市场 - 产业发展 - 研究报告 - 中国 Ⅳ.①G124

中国版本图书馆CIP数据核字（2018）第085872号

中国演艺市场发展报告

主　　编 / 李小牧　朱克宁
执行主编 / 李嘉珊　潘　燕

出 版 人 / 谢寿光
项目统筹 / 蔡继辉　任文武
责任编辑 / 杨　雪

出　　版 / 社会科学文献出版社·区域发展出版中心（010）59367143
　　　　　　地址：北京市北三环中路甲29号院华龙大厦　邮编：100029
　　　　　　网址：www.ssap.com.cn
发　　行 / 市场营销中心（010）59367081　59367018
印　　装 / 三河市尚艺印装有限公司

规　　格 / 开　本：787mm×1092mm　1/16
　　　　　　印　张：13.25　字　数：192千字
版　　次 / 2018年5月第1版　2018年5月第1次印刷
书　　号 / ISBN 978-7-5201-2661-8
定　　价 / 78.00元

本书如有印装质量问题，请与读者服务中心（010-59367028）联系